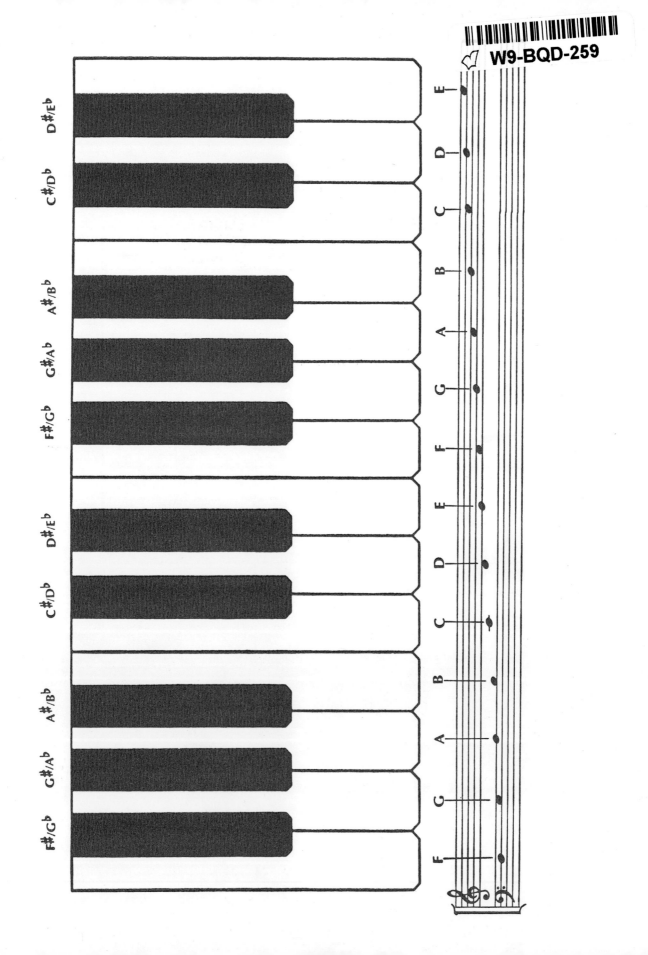

World of Music

Carmen E. Culp • Lawrence Eisman
Mary E. Hoffman
Authors

Carmino Ravosa • Phyllis Weikart
Theme Musical   Movement

Darrell Bledsoe
Producer, Vocal Recordings

Silver Burdett & Ginn
Morristown, NJ • Needham, MA
Atlanta, GA • Cincinnati, OH • Dallas, TX • Menlo Park, CA • Deerfield, IL

ISBN 0-382-07053-4

Contents

Performing Music 128

MUSIC FOR LIVING

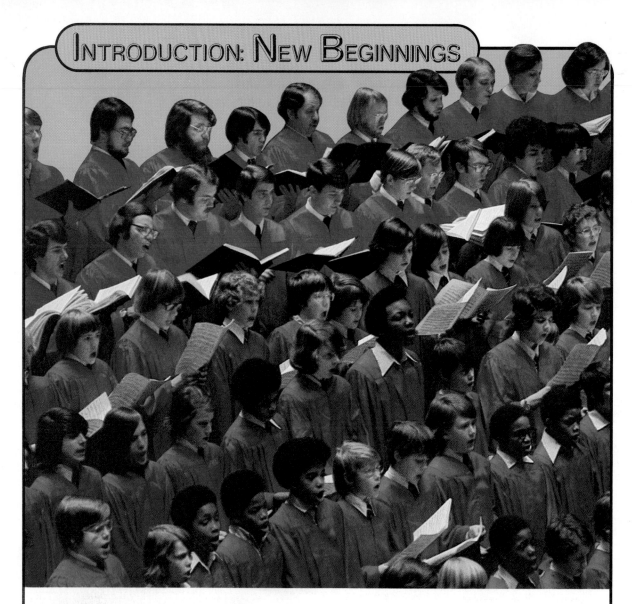

Collage of Singers

People sing in many ways. Some sing in church or synagogue choirs. Others <u>lead</u> those choirs or act as soloists. You can probably name a dozen or more of your favorite rock singers. Many listeners enjoy performers who sing in one of the Hispanic or country-western styles.

Even if you never become a famous singer yourself, you can still enjoy the fun of making music with your own voice. On the next three pages are some songs of different kinds. "Side by Side," on page 5, is a song that was popular a few years ago. "Sinner Man," on page 6, is an up-tempo black spiritual, and "Yesterday," on page 7, is a soft-rock ballad made famous by the Beatles. Sing these songs with your classmates—side by side.

Side by Side

Words and Music by Harry Woods

Oh! We ain't got a bar-rel of mon-ey, May-be we're rag-ged and
Don't know what's com-in' to - mor-row, May-be it's trou-ble and

fun-ny, But we'll trav-el a-long_ sing-in' a song_ side by side.
sor-row, But we'll trav-el the road_ shar-in' our load_ side by side.

Through all kinds of weath-er, what if the sky should fall?____ Just as

long as we're to-geth-er, it does-n't mat-ter at all;____

When they've all had their quar-rels and part-ed, We'll be the same as we

started, Just trav-'lin' a-long_ sing-in' a song_ side by

side.____ sing-in' a song_ side by side._____

Sinner Man

Black Spiritual   **Arranged by Lawrence Eisman**

(Part 1)

1. Oh, sin - ner man, where ___ you gon - na run to?
2. Run to the moon, "Moon, ___ won't you hide me?"
3. Lord says, "Sin - ner man, the moon - 'll be a - bleed - in'."

(Part 2)

(Verses 2 and 4) 1. Run, run, ___ run, sin - ner man;
(Verse 5) 2. Pray, pray, ___ pray, sin - ner man;

(Part 1)

Oh, sin - ner man, where ___ you gon - na run to? Oh, sin - ner man, where ___
Run to the sea, "Sea, ___ won't you hide me?" Run to the sun, "Sun, ___
Lord says, "Sin - ner man, the sea - 'll be a - sink - in'." Lord says, "Sin - ner man, the

(Part 2)

Run, run, ___ run, sin - ner man; Run, run, ___
Pray, pray, ___ pray, sin - ner man; Pray, pray, ___

(Part 1)

Last time

___ you gon - na run to, On, on that day? On,
___ won't you hide me, On, on that day?" On,
sun - 'll be a - freez - in', On, on that day."

(Part 2)

run, sin - ner man, On, on ___ a - that day. On,
pray, sin - ner man, On, on ___ a - that day.

(Part 1)

on that day. ___

(Part 2)

on that day. ___

4. Run to the Lord,
"Lord, won't you hide me?"
"On, on that day?" *(3 times)*

5. Lord says, "Sinner man,
you shoulda been a-prayin'!"
"On, on that day!" *(3 times)*

6

Yesterday ①

Words and Music by John Lennon and Paul McCartney

Yes - ter - day, all my trou - bles seemed so far a - way,
Sud - den - ly, I'm not half the man I used to be,

Now it looks as though they're here to stay, _ Oh, I be - lieve _ in
There's a shad-ow hang - ing o - ver me, _ Oh, yes - ter - day _ came

yes - ter - day. _ Why she had to go I don't know, she would-n't say.
sud - den - ly. _

I said some-thing wrong, now I long for yes - ter - day. _

Yes - ter - day, love was such an eas - y game to play,

Now I need a place to hide a - way, _ Oh, I be - lieve _ in

1. **2.**

rall.

yes - ter - day. _ yes - ter - day. _ Oh, I be - lieve in yes-ter - day. _

Music to Start the Show!

 Star Wars Theme (excerpt) . . . . Williams

Aretha Franklin sings the national anthem before the umpire shouts "Play Ball!" to allow the baseball game to begin. And every moviegoer thrills to the opening music of his or her favorite film— perhaps *Gone with the Wind,* or *Star Wars,* or *Rocky.*

Listen to the *Star Wars* theme again. As you listen to it, look at the chart below. In Column A you will find one list of descriptive words. In Column B you see another list. It isn't hard to see that the two columns are, in general, opposite in feeling. As you listen, decide which column best reflects the feeling of the music from *Star Wars.*

 Star Wars Theme (excerpt) . . . . Williams

Column A	Column B
Energetic	Relaxed
Adventurous	Easy
Strongly rhythmic	Gently rhythmic
Firm beat	Beat is not well defined
Loud dynamic	Soft dynamic
Stately tempo	Fast tempo
Brassy tone color	Strings and woodwinds predominate
Melody has many leaps	Melody moves mostly by step

Listen to some selections from other overtures or opening theme music. What words in the two columns can be used to describe these "openers"? Are there any other descriptive words you could add?

 Opening Themes

> *Carmen,* "Prelude" (excerpt). . . . . .Bizet
> *1776,* "Overture" (excerpt) . . . . Edwards
> *Also sprach Zarathustra* (as used in *2001—A Space Odyssey*) (excerpt) . . . . .Strauss

Talking It Out—Musically, That Is

Music can often reflect the personality of a person, or of two people in a dialogue. As you listen to these musical conversations, what do you imagine the two people to be like? What might they be saying to each other? What kinds of instruments are used to create these musical personalities? Can you match the conversationalists with their pictures?

 Musical Conversations

> *Pictures at an Exhibition,* "Samuel Goldenberg and Schmuyle" (excerpt)...................Mussorgsky
> *Mother Goose Suite,* "Beauty and the Beast" (excerpt) ....Ravel

Thank Goodness for Noah!

According to the story, if it hadn't been for Noah, there would be no animals around today—and that means a lot of musical pieces about them wouldn't have been composed. What a loss! Here are four musical descriptions of animals. Which music goes with which picture below? There is one more animal, but its picture is not here. This is the mystery animal. Can you tell what it is just from the music?

Musical Animals

The Waltzing Cat . . . . Anderson
Five Miniatures, "Mosquito Dance" . . . . White
Flight of the Bumblebee . . . . Rimsky-Korsakov
The Mystery Animal

Moods and Feelings

Have you ever found your mood changing as you listen to music?
Listen to the song "Scarborough Fair" in three versions. Each
version suggests a different mood. Don't worry if the mood you feel
doesn't exactly match your neighbor's. That's perfectly normal.

 Scarborough Fair (three versions)...... Traditional

Moods and Music

Probably no other art can suggest moods and feelings the way music
can. Listen to these musical excerpts and look at the words below.
How does the music suggest the mood or feeling of each word?

 Mood Music

Noble   *Boris Godunov,* "Coronation Scene"
(excerpt) .... Mussorgsky

desolate   *Isle of the Dead* (excerpt).... Rachmaninoff

   *La Gioconda,* "Dance of the Hours
(Galop)" (excerpt) .... Ponchielli

DRAMATIC   *Prince Igor,* "Polovtsian Dances"
(excerpt) .... Borodin

light   *Music for Strings, Percussion, and
Celesta* (excerpt) .... Bartók

   *Gaîté Parisienne,* "Can Can" (excerpt) .....
.... Offenbach

It All Depends on Your Viewpoint

Sometimes, more than one composer may write a descriptive piece about the same subject. Swans, sunrises, and storms have always been popular objects of inspiration.

Here are some well-known examples of the ways in which different composers have treated the same subjects. Before you listen to them, take a piece of paper and write the words *similarities* and *differences* at the top of the page. As you listen, jot down the things you hear in each piece that make it similar to the others, and the things that make it different from them. Some similarities might be mood, tempo (although this could be a difference), and obviously, subject matter. Differences might also include the kinds of instruments used, the dynamics (loud and soft), the meter, and the length of the piece.

 Likes and Differences Montage

Swan

The Swan of Tuonela (excerpt) . . . . Sibelius
Carnival of the Animals, "The Swan" (excerpt) . . . . . Saint-Saëns

Sunrise

Daphnis and Chloé (excerpt) . . . . Ravel
Grand Canyon Suite, "Sunrise" (excerpt) . . . . . Grofé

Storm

Grand Canyon Suite, "Cloudburst" (excerpt) . . Grofé
William Tell, "Overture" (excerpt) . . . . Rossini

Winding Up the Story

Picture This Scenario:

A group of people from a small town are in the "big city." The street is long, deserted, and quiet. They walk slowly, apprehensively, fearing the unknown. One lady clutches the arm of a man; another grips her handbag with both hands; two ladies link arms. No sound is made; eyes dart about in fear. One man nervously glances behind, while another man compulsively checks his wallet; a third man talks and laughs to conceal his fears. They approach a corner, when suddenly, the group is confronted with . . .
(music up)

Music up? Of course. How can you have the climax of a suspenseful scene without appropriate music? There's one small detail. We don't know what's around that corner! Knowing what's around that corner will tell us what kind of music we need to underscore it.

You Complete the Story

You have heard quite a bit of music in this lesson. Almost any piece could provide an appropriate musical ending to the story, depending on what you decide is around that corner. Here are three suggestions for the mood of whatever is around the corner. With your classmates, choose one and then choose music to fit it. You might then dramatize the end of the story. Make it fun!

Ending No. 1—festive

Ending No. 2—desolate

Ending No. 3—noble

Now—look around the corner to see. . . . .

A Drop of Drama

Have you ever watched a comedy or
drama on television?

Very often music is used to enhance and clarify the mood of the dialogue.
When radio dramas began to be broadcast many years ago, the electronic organ
was used. Today most television dramas use a full orchestra or a synthesizer.

Did you know that music, along with the actors' change in vocal
inflection, can alter the mood of the dialogue in a play? Listen to this
short dialogue without music. Then you will hear it done in three
different ways. Each time the actors will change their vocal inflections,
and the synthesizer will underscore the mood of the dialogue.

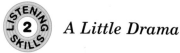 *A Little Drama*

SHE: I never expected to see you here.
HE: Why not? I told you I wouldn't change my plans.

How do the musical elements—the melody, the rhythm, the
harmony—work to change the mood of the dialogue each time? Do
you think the music increased *your* reaction to the "feeling" of the
drama? Remember, if you felt no change of mood, that's normal. Music
can suggest a mood, but cannot necessarily put the listener in that mood.

Mystery, Adventure, Fun (Musically Speaking)

Look at these scenes. Now listen to some music selected to describe these scenes. Can you match the music to the pictures? How does the music tell you about the pictures?

LISTENING SKILLS 2 *Background Music Montage*

Silent Movie

Have you ever turned down the audio on your TV set and watched the picture without sound? Until sound movies were introduced in 1928, that is exactly what audiences in motion picture theaters had to do. Many of these "silents"—such as *The Gold Rush, Intolerance,* and *Orphans of the Storm*—are still considered motion picture classics.

Almost every movie theater had a pianist or an organist, whose job was to provide music to enhance the story shown on the screen. These keyboard artists often used compositions by well-known composers to help create an emotional response in the audience, who sat in rapt attention before the flickering, soundless images.

You and Your Silent Movie

You can make your own silent-movie melodrama. Listen to this music played on the piano. Follow the script on page 19. Each time the tempo or the mood changes, you have moved into the next part of the script. Audiences in a melodrama feel perfectly free to shout "hooray" for the hero, to hiss the villain, and to sigh for the heroine. And here are the characters!

The Old Farmhouse

1. Sweet, innocent Little Nell Golightly floats through the flower garden in the country, gracefully picking flowers, communicating with the birds and butterflies, and thinking of Henry.

2. Suddenly, Mother Gertrude Golightly calls to her in fear. Little Nell rushes to the house and stands trembling on the porch with Mother, as Phineas P. Villainous stealthily approaches. He is a vile man!

3. He twirls his mustache in evil glee as he demands that Mother and Nell pay the mortgage on the house. Otherwise he will foreclose and throw them out. His deadline is one hour away.

4. The ladies fall to their knees, sobbing. Phineas shuns them in their helplessness. As they plead, he informs them that there *is* a way to save the farm. Little Nell must become his bride! Mother faints, and Nell runs to aid her.

5. Phineas lowers the brim of his hat, dramatically flings his cloak about himself, and holds the mortgage high. Pointing a sinister finger at Little Nell and pulling his watch from a pocket, he reminds her of the deadline and slithers off. Alone, Little Nell and her mother empty a bowl of a few coins—their only savings. They are doomed! It's already fifteen minutes to one! Little Nell dejectedly rises and tearfully bids Mother farewell as Villainous's car is heard approaching. A trembling Little Nell and her sobbing mother slowly walk out onto the porch.

6. Nell, head bowed, is about to enter the car when—hark! The sound of another auto is heard. It is Henry Heartenmuscle! He has brought Little Nell's inheritance from her uncle, as well as proof that Phineas holds a forged deed to the Golightly property! "Curses, foiled again!" mutters Phineas as he makes a hasty exit.

7. Heavenly happiness reigns as Little Nell falls into Henry's strong arms. Henry proposes to Little Nell. She accepts. Mother smiles peacefully. The sun is shining once again on "The Old Farmhouse."

CHAPTER 2—STYLE THEN AND NOW

Style–What Is It?

There are hat styles, clothing styles, automobile styles. There are styles of music, too: Renaissance (REHN uh sah[n]s) style, Classic style, Romantic style, folk style, rock style. What *is* style?

The two cars above are different in the way they look, even though they are both automobiles. How do they differ in appearance?

Now listen to two songs about New York. Think about how they are alike and yet different. Are the harmonies different? The melodies? The rhythm?

The Sidewalks of New York 🔴

Words and Music by Charles B. Lawlor and James W. Blake

East side, West side, all a - round the town, _____

The tots sang "ring _ a - ros - ie," "Lon - don Bridge is fall - ing down." _____

Boys and girls to - geth - er, _____ me and Ma - mie O' - Rourke, _____

Tripped the light _ fan - tas - tic on the side-walks of New York. _____

New York, New York ②

Words by Fred Ebb   Music by John Kander

Start spread-in' the news, I'm leav-in' to - day, I want to be a part _ of it: New York, New York. These vag - a-bond shoes are long-ing to stray, And step a - round the heart _ of it: New York, New York. I want to wake up in the cit-y that does -n't sleep to find I'm king of the hill, I'm top of the heap. my lit-tle-town blues are melt-ing a - way, I'll make a brand new start _ of it in old New York. _ If I can make it __ there, __ I'll _ make it an - y - where, __ It's up to

1. you, New York, New York. Come on, come Start spread-in' the

2. through New York, New York. _

The Parts That Make Up Style

Style is what gives an object, a song, a story, a movie—even a whole period of history—its look or sound or feel. Some of the visible parts of an automobile, for example, are its general body shape, its four wheels, its exhaust pipe, its front grille, its bumper, and its hood design. Both cars on page 20 have all these parts, but there is something different about the shape of each part. The shapes give the cars different "looks" overall. They represent two different *styles*.

Styles of Marches

Let's talk about styles in music. You heard the differences in style between "The Sidewalks of New York" and "New York, New York."

Have you ever watched a band at a football game or in a parade? If you have, you probably heard one of the world's favorite musical forms—the march. Marches have been written and played since ancient times, mostly to accompany military units on the move.

Playing with a Band

Like the automobile, all marches are the same in their basic make-up. But just as the different parts of the automobile change in style, so can the parts of a march—its tempo, dynamic level, harmonies, rhythms, and melody.

As you listen to these marches, listen for the things that make them different in style from one another. Match them to the pictures on this page.

LISTENING SKILLS 2

Styles of Marches

Semper Fideles . . . . Sousa
Aida, "Grand March" . . Verdi
*When the Saints Go
Marching In* . . . . . Traditional

From Now to Then

Listen to "When the Saints Go Marching In" one more time.

 When the Saints Go Marching In . . Traditional

Now listen to this piece performed by an ensemble playing instruments from long ago.

 Canzona . . . . Maschera

The second piece is a lively composition from long ago—the sixteenth century, to be exact. That time in history is called the Renaissance. Do you hear any similarity between *Canzona* and our old friend *the Saints*? They are both very rhythmic pieces, with a great deal of jazzy syncopation. They are both loud and fast. How are they different? The most obvious difference is in the instruments.

24

The instrument on the left in each pair below is used in *Canzona;* the one on the right is used in *the Saints*. Each instrument on the right is a modern relative of the one on the left.

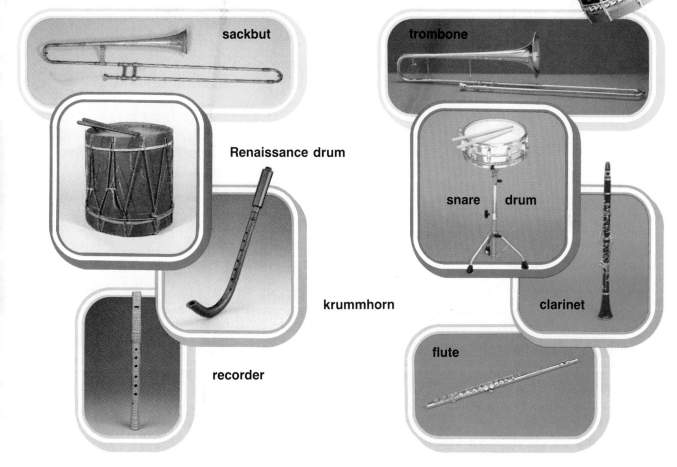

sackbut

trombone

Renaissance drum

snare   drum

krummhorn

clarinet

recorder

flute

Very few of our modern-day instruments have developed without forebears. The synthesizer is one of the few exceptions. What instruments might develop out of the instruments we know today?

The Renaissance — What's in a Name?

Cantoria, **right side panel. Boys Singing Holding Music Scroll. Luca della Robbia.**

Do you know what *Renaissance* means? This impressive word comes from the French word *naissance,* meaning "birth." The prefix *re-* makes the meaning "a new birth," or "rebirth." But rebirth of what?

For many centuries the church in the West had kept alive many of the Greek and Roman traditions in knowledge, music, and art. From about 1450, many individuals, apart from the church, began to gather wealth and gain position. Their new leisure time allowed them to study Greek and Roman culture and thinking on their own. These lay people—merchants and professionals (doctors, lawyers, and so forth)—began to broaden their interests to include popular as well as church music and art. It was this "rebirth" of interest in the enduring values of Greek and Roman culture, that gave rise to the term *Renaissance.* Indeed, many have called the Renaissance the beginning of modern society. From 1450 until now—that's a long modern history.

Singing in the Renaissance

Have you ever sung a popular song with your family? Have you ever sung rounds at home? The habit of singing at home was a truly happy part of Renaissance life.

Catches (from the Italian word *caccia,* meaning "chase") were very popular because they were easy to sing and everyone got to sing melody. That is because the catch is a kind of round. But it is a round with a sense of humor. Sing "Sing Out" and see if you can discover the joke. You may want to listen to it on the recording first.

Sing Out

Words by Sir Thomas Crickley   Music Anonymous

When you have learned "Sing Out," add the following part on tambourine. You may use any other percussion instrument, but the tambourine is a very appropriate instrument because it was so popular during the Renaissance. The tambourine helps to give "Sing Out" its Renaissance style.

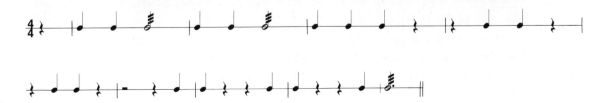

Solo Voices in the Renaissance

"Sing Out" is a lighthearted catch with a joke in it. It has to be sung by several voices together to make it "work." The Renaissance also saw a new interest in solo voices. The painting below shows a young woman of the period preparing to play a lute and sing.

The Lute Player
Orazio Gentileschi.

Renaissance Music Was Never Behind Bars

Listen again to *When the Saints Go Marching In*. See if you can keep time to the meter.

2 *When the Saints Go Marching In* . . . . **Traditional**

It is easy to keep time to this music, isn't it? *Saints* is in a meter of 2. (You probably remember that in $\frac{2}{4}$ meter there are two beats in each measure and that a quarter note [♩] equals one beat.) Now sing, or listen to "My Joy Would Grow in Measure." Try to keep time to the meter as you listen. Notice that there are *two* solo voices.

My Joy Would Grow in Measure

15th-Century Folk Song from Germany   English Words by Ruth Martin

Word Painting and Sound Effects

Many Renaissance composers tried to "paint" the words of the text in sound. Sometimes obvious, at other times more subtle, the use of word painting was almost always there.

You may never have heard of "The Battle of Marignan," but it was one of the big hits of the Renaissance. Even today it is often found on concert programs by choral groups. In it the chorus imitates the sounds of battle. As each number is called, look at the chart below to see how the battle progresses. Can you hear the meter change to $\frac{6}{8}$ in calls 3 and 5? You may remember that $\frac{6}{8}$ means there are six beats in a measure with the eighth note ($\eighthnote$) standing for one beat. Sometimes $\frac{6}{8}$ feels like a measure of two beats with each beat divided into three eighths.

Call Chart 1

 2 *The Battle of Marignan* . . . . Jannequin

The Preparation for Battle

1 The chorus calls to hear about the battle of Marignan.

2 The chorus imitates the fifes.

3 The soldiers mount their horses and canter away. $(\frac{6}{8})$

4 They cry out to defeat the enemy.

5 They call for the trumpets. $(\frac{6}{8})$

The Battle

6 The chorus imitates drums and bugles, swirling and whirling of battle.

7 A lyric passage calls for aid to the injured.

8 The chorus imitates the boom! boom! of the cannons, and the swirling of battle, bugles, and rifle fire.

The Victory

9 There are cries of "Defeat them! Beat them! They are lost!" and finally, "Victory!" (*Victoire!*).

Polyphony—Many Voices (but One Style)

Choir of Angels
Hans Memling.

Polyphony—another jawbreaking word, pronounced puh LIHF uh nee. It comes from the Greek words meaning "many" (*poli*) "voices" (*phone*). Do you know the old favorite rounds "Are You Sleeping?," "Three Blind Mice," and "Row, Row, Row Your Boat"? Three groups can sing these songs together.

Divide your class into three groups. Group 1 sings "Are You Sleeping?" beginning on the note D.
- The second time through, group 2 will join in with "Three Blind Mice," beginning on F♯.
- Finally, group 3 joins in with "Row, Row, Row Your Boat," beginning on D. Group 3 must sing "Row, Row" twice to make it fit the other two rounds.

Although songs you can sing together are called "partner songs," what results is *polyphony*—many voices singing many different things. Renaissance composers loved polyphony, especially in serious works with a sacred character. Very often it is possible to recognize the style of the Renaissance just by the polyphonic character of the music.

Listen to "Non Nobis, Domine" on page 32. After you have heard it a few times, learn to sing it. The pronunciation of the Latin words is printed in blue. Can you hear the imitation in the voices?

31

Non Nobis, Domine

Words from Psalm 115   **Music by William Byrd**

Music in the Church

While much music took on a secular character during the Renaissance, the Church was still the most important caretaker of religious music, as it had been for centuries. This music, while devotional in nature, went beyond its religious purpose to become music that could be enjoyed for its own sake, without any religious intent on the part of the listener. ("Non Nobis, Domine" is just one example of this.) Even so, in a church-service setting, it is not usually proper to applaud. The audience listens to the music quietly and reverently. Some composers devoted most of their labor to producing music for the church. Such a man was Giovanni Pierluigi da Palestrina.

Palestrina—the Standard Setter

While Palestrina wrote "O Bone Jesu" in four parts—soprano, alto, tenor, bass—the version here is for soprano, alto, and tenor only.

O Bone Jesu

Giovanni Pierluigi da Palestrina   Arranged by Mary H. Hoffman

Lyrics under the music:

S: mi - sti nos san - gui - ne tu - o pre -
mee - stee nohs sahn - gwee - nay too - oh pray -

A: mi - sti nos san - gui - ne tu - o pre -

T: mi - sti nos san - gui - ne tu - o pre -

S: ti - o - sis - si - mo.
tsee - oh - sees - see - moh

A: ti - o - sis - si - mo.

T: ti - o - sis - si - mo.

Palestrina took his last name from his birthplace in Italy. Many feel that his music is the best and most typical of Renaissance polyphonic church music. He conducted many choirs in Rome, including the choir of St. John Lateran, the church of the bishop of Rome (the pope). He was in the forefront when choral music underwent serious reform.

Giovanni Pierluigi da Palestrina
(1525–1594)

The Wandering Minstrel

Allan-a-Dale is a minstrel in the Robin Hood stories. Some of the minstrels of the twentieth century are Burl Ives, Pete Seeger, Lionel Ritchie, and Linda Ronstadt. As they tour from town to town, they take music to the people.

In the Middle Ages, minstrels—usually men but sometimes women as well—went from town to town singing ballads they had made up about current events. It was the only way news could be broadcast in those days. By the Renaissance times, minstrels had become a unique kind of entertainer. They must have seemed like "one-man bands." They played flute and drum at the same time. A minstrel would hold a three-holed flute in the left hand, using three fingers to cover the holes when necessary, and hang a small drum from the little finger with a piece of string. With a mallet in the right hand, the minstrel played the drum.

36

Dances, Dances, Dances

Every age has had its dances. The Renaissance was no exception.
While the twentieth century has produced its Charleston, fox-trot,
jitterbug, shag, swim, rumba, and funky chicken, the Renaissance
had its pavane, galliard, and saltarello—each era different in its
dance style.

One lively Renaissance dance was the *bransle* (pronounced "brawl,"
"BRAN s'l," or "BRAN uhl"). Although there is no connection, it might
seem as if our modern English word *brawl* came from this dance,
described as vigorously done, with a great deal of stamping and
jumping. Wind instruments usually accompanied the bransle, since
their extra power was needed to be heard over the racket!

Bransle . . . . .Attaignant

Ladies and gentlemen of the Renaissance had their slow dances, too.
Listen to this pavane, as played by a consort, or group, of four
recorders.

Si pas souffrir. . . . . .Susato

Ball Given at the Court of Henry III, 16th Century French School.
Cliché des Musées Nationaux, Paris (Louvre)

Music in the Baroque Period

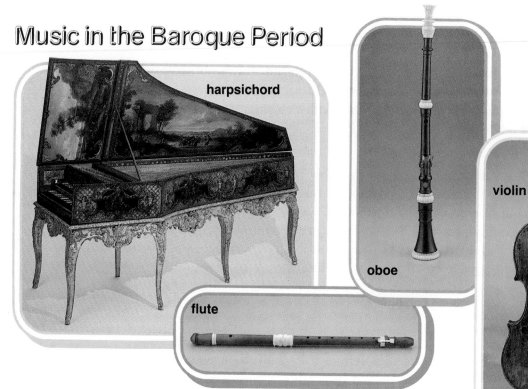

harpsichord

oboe

flute

violin

Violin: The Metropolitan Museum of Art.
Gift of Mrs. Evelyn Stark. 1974. (1974.229)

Did you play a recorder when you were younger? Perhaps you still play one. The recorder is an instrument that is very ancient. You heard recorders playing a pavane. Listen to this performance of a recorder piece from the Baroque period and try to think how the piece is different from the pavane.

Concerto in C Major for Sopranino Recorder, Harpsichord, and Strings, Movement 1......Vivaldi

Could you hear any difference in style between the two pieces—the pavane and the recorder concerto? The charts below show you some of the differences in style.

Renaissance	Baroque
1 Only recorders.	1 Adds harpsichord.
2 Phrases not of equal length.	2 All phrases of equal length.
3 Smooth rhythm.	3 Rhythm has a "typewriter" quality.
4 Melodies repeat.	4 Melodies do not exactly repeat. Each phrase grows out of the one before it.

Call Chart 2

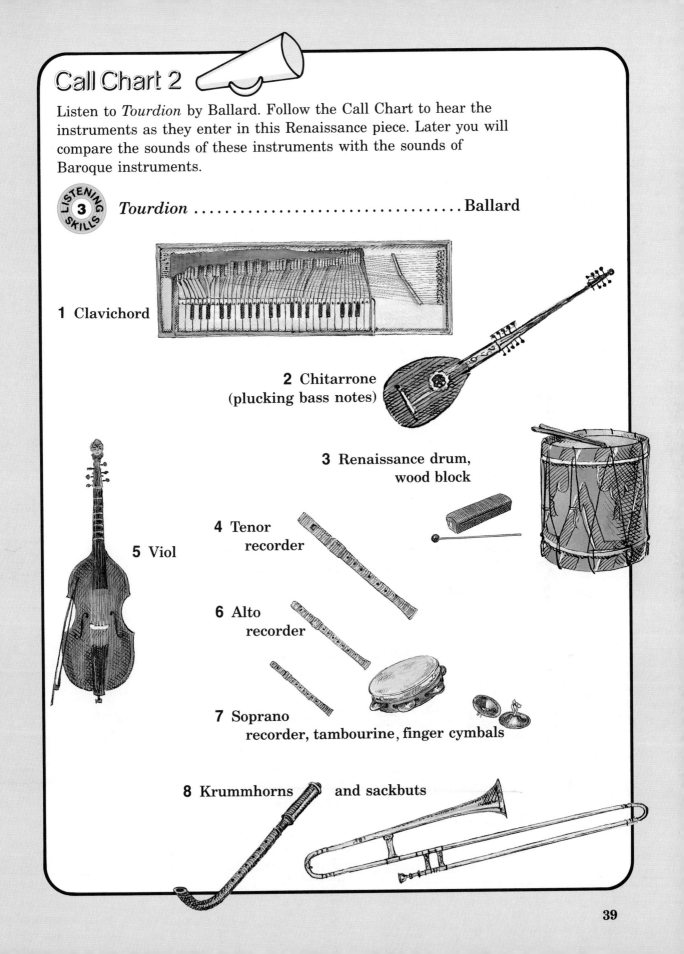

Listen to *Tourdion* by Ballard. Follow the Call Chart to hear the instruments as they enter in this Renaissance piece. Later you will compare the sounds of these instruments with the sounds of Baroque instruments.

3 *Tourdion* . . . . Ballard

1 Clavichord

2 Chitarrone
(plucking bass notes)

3 Renaissance drum,
wood block

5 Viol

4 Tenor
recorder

6 Alto
recorder

7 Soprano
recorder, tambourine, finger cymbals

8 Krummhorns   and sackbuts

Enter the Strings

Listen to J. S. Bach's *Brandenburg Concerto No. 3*. As you listen, ask yourself what kinds of instruments are in the orchestra.

3 *Brandenburg Concerto No. 3*, Movement 1 . . . . . Bach

As you listened to Bach's concerto, what instruments did you hear most? If you said strings, you were right! (Harpsichord, too.)

The Four Seasons

Vivaldi wrote many works for string orchestra. Among them was a set of four string concertos called *The Four Seasons*. In the last movement of the "Autumn" concerto, a movement called THE HUNT, Vivaldi used *tone painting* to suggest an autumn hunt and the sounds that accompany it. The orchestra is composed entirely of string instruments, harpsichord, and there is one violin soloist. Here is a line score for you to follow as you listen. The yellow bands show the *tutti,* or full-orchestra, passages; the blue bands show the music played by the violin soloist.

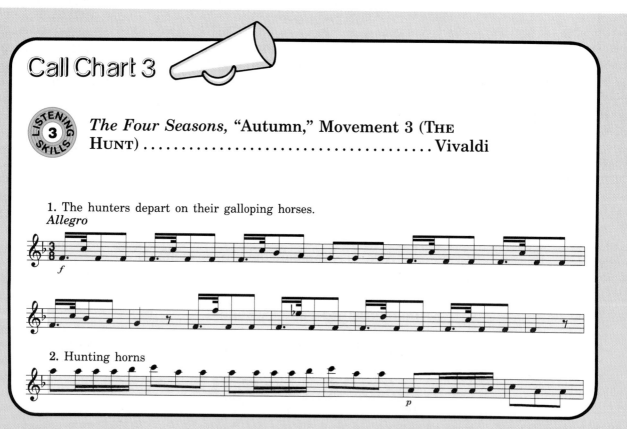

Call Chart 3

3 *The Four Seasons,* "Autumn," Movement 3 (THE HUNT) . . . . Vivaldi

1. The hunters depart on their galloping horses.
Allegro

2. Hunting horns

3. Fanfares in solo violin (hunting horns)

4. Galloping horses

5. Fanfares

6. The wild game flees and hunters pursue.

7. The game, frightened by the din of gunfire, runs and leaps.

8. The chase continues.

42

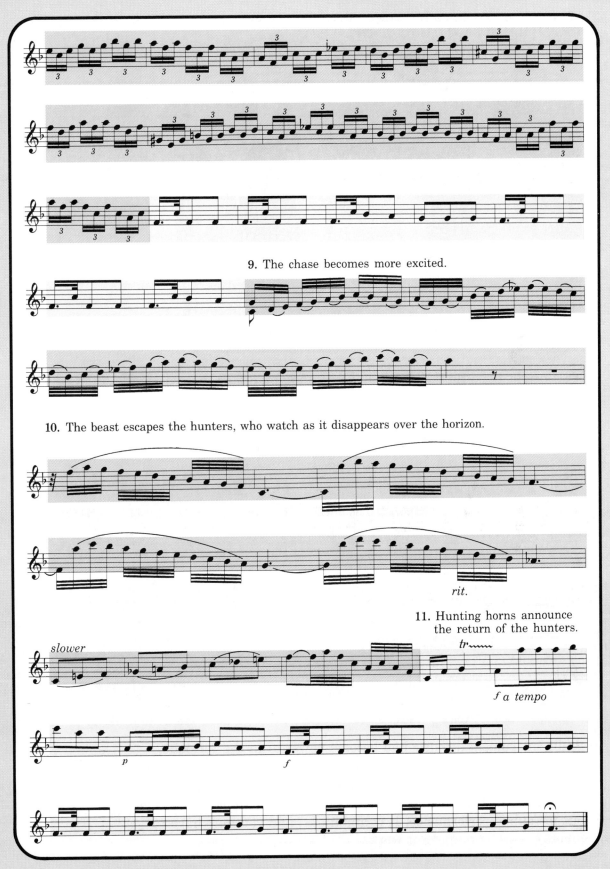

9. The chase becomes more excited.

10. The beast escapes the hunters, who watch as it disappears over the horizon.

rit.

11. Hunting horns announce the return of the hunters.

slower

f a tempo

p

f

Rounding Off the Baroque

This bright little Baroque round can be sung by either three or six voices. Try learning it as a three-part round, then as a six-part round.

Where There Is Gladness

Words by Sir Thomas Crickly   Music by Philip Hayes

While instrumental music had become powerful in the Baroque, vocal music had not been neglected. People still wanted to sing, and sing they did! The round "Halleluja" is one of the many rounds written not just for singing at home, as was the Renaissance catch, but for public performance. It is ambitious, and you may have to practice a while to make it work.

Halleluja

Music by Philip Hayes

One of the new vocal forms to arise during the Baroque was the *oratorio*. There is one oratorio that you can hardly fail to miss during the month of December, when it is performed in thousands of schools, churches, and concert halls, and on radio and TV. It is *Messiah,* by George Frideric Handel. Some of you may even have sung parts of it, especially the famous chorus, "Hallelujah."

Listen for the way *Hallelujah!* is tossed back and forth from voice to voice, and the way one voice sings *For the Lord God omnipotent reigneth* while the other voice sings *Hallelujah!* This melody-against-melody style is typical of the kind of polyphony (now called *counterpoint*) developed by Baroque composers.

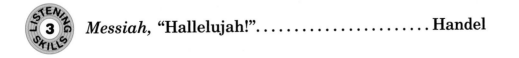 *Messiah,* "Hallelujah!"..................Handel

Music of the Classic Period

"Equality" is a good word to describe the term *classic*. When people think of architecture, music, painting, or furniture as classic, they think of equality of parts, balance of form, and simplicity of the whole. "Equality" is a song from the Classic period that shows equality and balance.

Equality 3

English Words by Georg von Sudland Music by Joseph Haydn

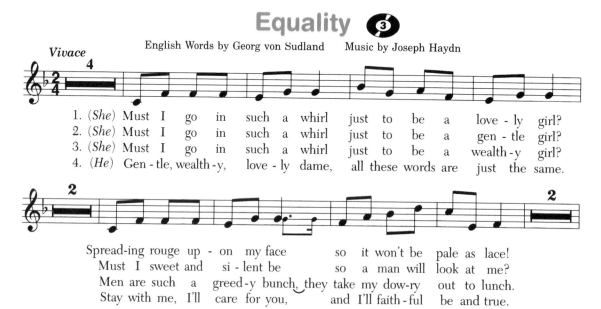

Vivace

1. (*She*) Must I go in such a whirl just to be a love-ly girl?
2. (*She*) Must I go in such a whirl just to be a gen-tle girl?
3. (*She*) Must I go in such a whirl just to be a wealth-y girl?
4. (*He*) Gen-tle, wealth-y, love-ly dame, all these words are just the same.

Spread-ing rouge up-on my face so it won't be pale as lace!
Must I sweet and si-lent be so a man will look at me?
Men are such a greed-y bunch, they take my dow-ry out to lunch.
Stay with me, I'll care for you, and I'll faith-ful be and true.

46

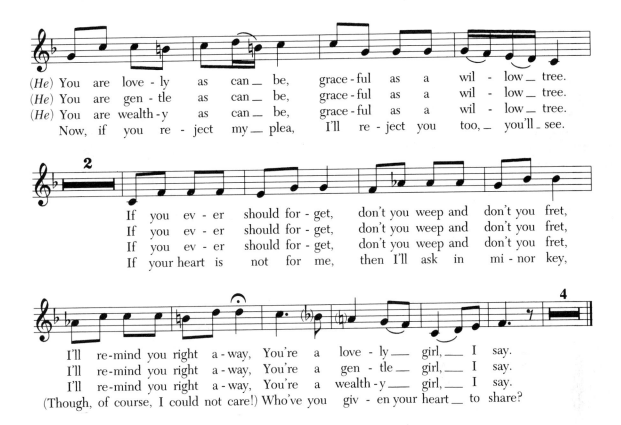

(He) You are love-ly as can — be, grace-ful as a wil - low — tree.
(He) You are gen-tle as can — be, grace-ful as a wil - low — tree.
(He) You are wealth-y as can — be, grace-ful as a wil - low — tree.
Now, if you re - ject my — plea, I'll re - ject you too, — you'll - see.

If you ev - er should for - get, don't you weep and don't you fret,
If you ev - er should for - get, don't you weep and don't you fret,
If you ev - er should for - get, don't you weep and don't you fret,
If your heart is not for me, then I'll ask in mi - nor key,

I'll re-mind you right a - way, You're a love - ly — girl, — I say.
I'll re-mind you right a - way, You're a gen - tle — girl, — I say.
I'll re-mind you right a - way, You're a wealth-y — girl, — I say.
(Though, of course, I could not care!) Who've you giv - en your heart — to share?

Think of the Baroque pieces you have heard and sung. How do they
compare in style with "Equality"? The chart below will help you
read those differences.

Baroque Pieces	"Equality"
1 Polyphonic.	1 Homophonic.
2 Complexity	2 Simplicity
3 Driving rhythm and many cross-rhythms	3 Rhythms are "square"
4 Harmonies change quickly, off and on every beat.	4 Harmonies change more slowly, usually one or two per measure.
5 Melodic phrases unfold from one another rather than repeat exactly.	5 Much melodic repetition.

Canon or Cannon?

Do you remember singing "Sing Out"? Do you remember the joke in that Renaissance catch? Composers of the Classic period also loved to joke and play games. One of the first things noticed in some Classic pieces is their sense of joy and fun. This round, or canon, is also a joke in that the composer made a pun on the words *canon* and *cannon*.

Cannons?

English Words by Georg von Sudland   Music by Antonio Salieri

This is not a song a-bout a can-non, not a can-non that is used to make as-sault up-on the en-e-my, for vic-to-ry in bat-tle. It's a gen - tle can - on that is pleas-ant to our hear-ing, One to set our hearts a-sing-ing and bring us all to-geth-er; One to set our hearts a-sing-ing and bring us all to -

49

The Classic Orchestra

fortepiano

oboe

violin

flute

Think of the instruments we have heard so far—how they looked, how they sounded. Do you remember the drastic change in sound from the Renaissance to the Baroque? The growth from the Baroque to the Classic period is not quite so dramatic, but even so, instruments were evolving into what would become our modern instruments.

Composers, too, were writing in new ways. When Baroque composers like Vivaldi and Bach wrote for wind instruments, they tended to use them as solo instruments. Listen to this movement from a symphony by Mozart, who many feel was the greatest composer of the Classic period. He used all the instruments pictured in the montage above. How did Mozart use the wind instruments in ways that are different from the Baroque composers?

Symphony No. 40 in G Minor, Movement 4 .. Mozart

As larger and larger concert halls were built, orchestras needed instruments that could play louder. Also, Classic composers began to include instruments that Baroque composers had not used, such as the trombone and the piccolo. Until the Classic period, those instruments had been used primarily in folk groups and dance ensembles.

50

A Balancing Act

A sense of balance—that's how we defined *classic*. In the older Baroque, music often raced forward with rarely an exact repetition of phrase, although whole sections might be repeated. The phrases seemed to tumble from one another, growing out of each other. In the Classic period, however, composers began to look for a sense of formal balance, or equality.

Wolfgang Amadeus Mozart—whose rivalry with Salieri (the composer of "Cannons") has been discussed in books, plays, movies, and operas—was a master of form. Mozart wrote music in all the major forms of the day: symphonies, concertos, operas, sonatas, string quartets, and even popular songs. His operas have a special spirit about them—the tragic ones containing deep meaning and the comic ones unleashing hilarious wit.

A Classic Overture

On page 52, there is a Call Chart for the overture to Mozart's comic opera, *The Marriage of Figaro.* In this overture, Mozart features the winds, brasses, and percussion as well as the basic corps of strings. Here are the basic themes as they will be heard in calls 1, 2, 6, 9, and 11. They will be played on piano.

The Marriage of Figaro themes

Call Chart 4

	SECTION	INSTRUMENTS	DYNAMICS
1	Theme A See page 51.	Strings and bassoons in low register	*pp*
2	Theme B See page 51.	Woodwinds and French horns, then full orchestra	*p ff*
3	Theme A repeated	Add flute and oboe to instruments in call 1	*p*
4	Theme B repeated	Same as call 2	*p ff*
5	Cadence Descending scales, then ascending scales and an abrupt stop.	Full orchestra	*alternating loud and soft*
6	Theme C See page 51.	Strings and woodwinds	*sforzando*
7	Theme C repeated	Same as call 6	*same as call 6*
8	Bridge to next theme Soft melody outlines a chord interspersed with loud chords in blocks.	Full orchestra	*soft and loud*
9	Theme D See page 51.	Full orchestra; melody in bassoons, violas, cellos, and string basses	*f*
10	Theme D repeated	Melody in violins, extension of melody in bassoon	*p*

	SECTION	INSTRUMENTS	DYNAMICS
11	Closing theme See page 51.	Strings, French horns, bassoon; melody in violins	*p*
12	Closing theme repeated	Add flute to melody.	*p*
13	Bridge to repeat of all of the above	Full orchestra	alternating loud and soft
14	Theme A followed by Theme B	Same as calls 1 and 2	same as calls 1 and 2
15	Theme A changed slightly	Full orchestra	*p f*
16	Theme C twice	Strings and woodwinds	sforzando
17	Bridge as in call 8	Full orchestra	soft and loud
18	Theme D twice	Same as calls 9 and 10	same as calls 9 and 10
19	Closing theme as in call 11 twice	Strings, woodwinds, French horns	*p*
20	Coda Ascending eighth note figures from Theme B	Strings, woodwinds, then full orchestra	*pp to f*

Music of the Romantic Period

Do your own thing! Be an individual! Live and express yourself freely and loudly! Write music for the popular culture! Sound like life in New York or San Francisco today? Yes, but that is also a good description of artistic life in the great European capitals from about 1820 to around 1900—an era called the Romantic period.

The Romantics Had Style

"Romantic" as a style does not mean mushy love scenes on TV or in the movies. Romantic style was marked by a lot of individual freedom, different harmonic ideas, new ways of building music (form), strong emotional appeal, a sense of the dramatic, a love for soaring melody, large orchestras with new instrumental colors as well as old instruments perfected to our modern standards. While the Classic composer loved order and form and wrote music that was only about music itself, the Romantic composer often wrote in forms that were rather loose, and the music was often about nonmusical subjects. Sharp clashes of dynamics, tempo, and mood prevailed.

The Romantic composer loved nature, was very devout and patriotic, and had a deep interest in the supernatural. It is no accident that two of the greatest horror novels, later made into many successful motion pictures, were Romantic novels. They were *Frankenstein,* by Mary Wollstonecraft Shelley, and *Dracula,* by Bram Stoker. The stories of the "fabricated man" and the bloodthirsty vampire were made-to-order for the Romantic public, thrilling the readers in the 1800s, just as they do the modern public today.

The Romantic Orchestra

Ghosts? The supernatural? Described with new instrumental colors? Composers in the nineteenth century had a vast array of tone colors to help them tell their stories. Do you remember listening to the final movement of "Autumn," from *The Four Seasons,* by Vivaldi? He gave us some idea of hunting horns and a chase through the fields and forests by using only string instruments! Had Vivaldi been a Romantic composer, what other instruments do you think he would have used in "Autumn"?

Some instruments that were available to the Romantic composer but not to Vivaldi in the Baroque period were the tuba, the contrabassoon, the piccolo, the trombone, and the piano.

A Ghostly Dance

The French composer Camille Saint-Saëns (ka MEE SA[N] SAH[N]) describes the program of his orchestral composition *Danse macabre* (dah[n]s ma KAHB).

It is night. The clock strikes midnight. We hear the ghost fiddler tune his strings, getting ready for the dance. Other ghosts leave their graves to begin the merry-making. The music moves faster and faster as the ghosts become more and more frenzied in their movements. Suddenly a rooster crows, heralding the dawn. The ghostly figures cannot survive the light of day and must stop their merry-making and steal back to their graves to lie in wait for another night of revelry.

In *Danse macabre* the solo violinist is asked to tune a string "out-of-tune." This helps to give that special "spooky" feeling to the piece. To understand and follow the story, listen to the music in *Call Chart 5* on page 57 and look at the pictures as each number is called.

Call Chart 5

57

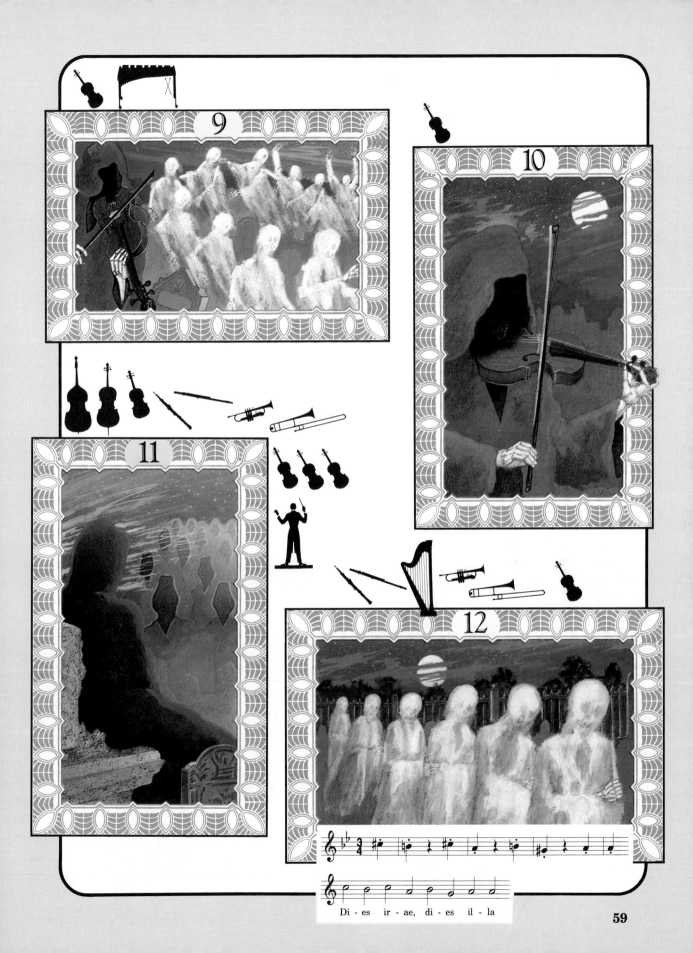

Di - es ir - ae, di - es il - la

59

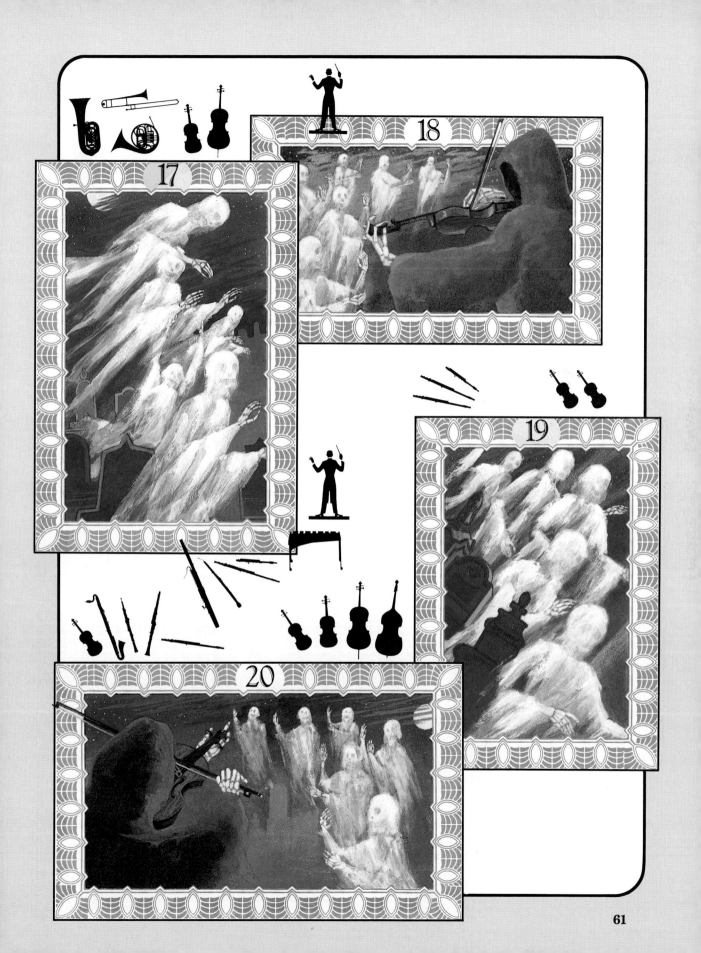

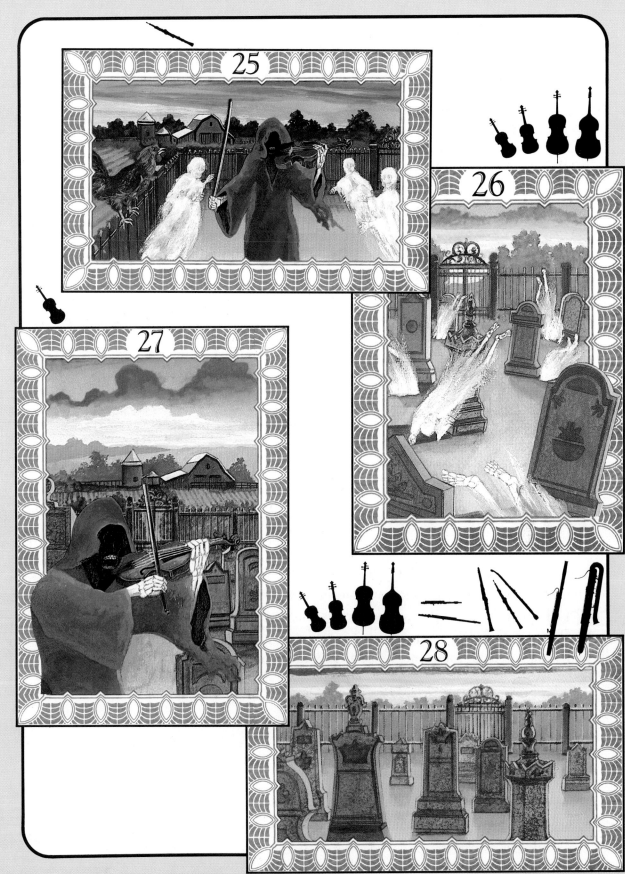

Marching On to a New Century—Our Own

The Major Scale

Take the bells and line them up as shown. Then play them up and down to hear their special sound.

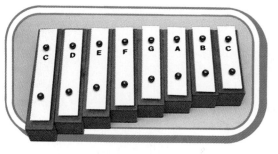

Probably you have sung, at some time or other, the "do re mi" scale.

C   D   E   F   G   A   B   C
do   re   mi   fa   sol la   ti   do

This scale is a *major scale*. Since the beginning of the Baroque period, composers have based most of their music on two scales—the major scale and the minor scale. What *is* a scale? A scale is a line of notes arranged in a pattern. Your teacher can play whole and half steps on the piano so you can hear the difference between them. The major scale is arranged in this pattern of whole and half steps.

⌊__⌋ = whole   ∨ = half

C   D   E   F   G   A   B   C

You can see there is a half step between E and F and between B and high C. It is this arrangement that gives the major scale its special sound.

No matter what note the major scale starts with, the pattern of half and whole steps is the same. Look at this major scale on D.

D   E   F♯   G   A   B   C♯   D

The pattern of half and whole steps is the same as in the major scale on C.

Many familiar pieces of music—folk songs, hymns, symphonies, rock songs—are based on the major scale. The song on page 65 is typical of the "major" sound.

We Shall Overcome

Traditional
New Words and Musical Arrangement by Zilphia Horton, Frank Hamilton, Guy Carawan, and Pete Seeger

(Sing harmony on 2nd verse only)

1. We shall o-ver-come,_____ We shall o-ver-come,_____
2. We'll walk hand in hand,_____ We'll walk hand in hand,_____

We shall o-ver-come some day._____ Oh,_____
We'll walk hand in hand some day._____

deep in my heart I do be-lieve,

We shall o-ver-come some day._____

Out of the Scale Come Chords

The chords used in accompanying or supporting a melody come from the scale on which the melody is based. Look at this major scale on C and the chords that are derived from it.

C D E F G A B C

Here is a part for you to play on bells or other instruments to go with the first verse of "We Shall Overcome." The names of the chords are written over them.

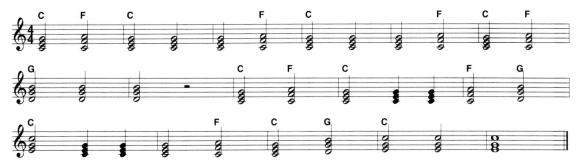

The Minor Scale

The second scale used by most composers is the *minor scale*.

Line up your bells again, but this time arrange them in this order.

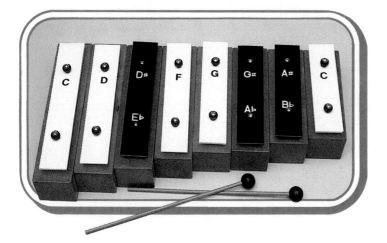

Play the bells in order up and down. The minor scale sounds very different from the major scale, doesn't it? That's because the pattern of whole and half steps has changed. Look at the minor scale as written on the staff, beginning on C.

Now the pattern has a half step between D and E♭, the second and third notes of the scale, and between G and A♭, the fifth and sixth notes. No matter what note the scale begins on, the pattern of half and whole steps is the same. For example, here is the minor scale on D.

TimeTunnel

James Roberts' rock composition, *TimeTunnel*, on page 67, is based on the minor scale. As you listen, be aware of the minor sound. Could you possibly sing the song in major? After listening, work out the bell parts on page 67 to play along with *TimeTunnel*. Do you see the sign in the fifth staff that looks like this: ✗ ? That means to repeat the measure before.

Impressionism

Do you ever wake up from a dream and try to remember what you dreamed? Perhaps in a daydream you tried to remember details of a place you had visited. The images were rather vague, weren't they?

It is hard to recapture such details. Probably all you could get would be an *impression* of the dream or the place.

Impression: Sunrise
Claude Monet.

In the late nineteenth century a French painter, Claude Monet (moh NAY), helped create a new style of painting called *Impressionism*. The movement took its name from Monet's revolutionary painting *Impression: Sunrise*. In the painting, the artist caught his subject as remembered from a dream or a daydream. The outlines are not clear, and the colors are muted. Some modern students of Monet's paintings say that the artist's "revolutionary" technique may have been the result of his poor eyesight—that he may simply have been recording the results of his own blurred visual perception. No matter what the cause, Monet created a style that would influence not only painting but literature and music as well.

Impressionism in Music

Musicians were not untouched by impressionism. The musician who first introduced impressionism in music was Claude Debussy (duh bew see), a French composer. Listen to this montage of impressionist pieces. How does this music differ from what you have heard before?

Impressionist Montage

Prelude to the Afternoon of a Faun (excerpt)....... ....Debussy
Gaspard de la nuit (excerpt)................Ravel
The Pleasure Dome of Kubla Khan (excerpt)..Griffes
Voiles (excerpt) ....Debussy

The last piece you heard, *Voiles* (pronounced "vwahl"), is a piano piece that uses a device closely associated with impressionism. That device is the *whole-tone* scale.

You remember that a scale is a pattern of whole and half steps. A whole-tone scale is precisely that—a pattern made entirely of whole steps. Line up your bells in this order.

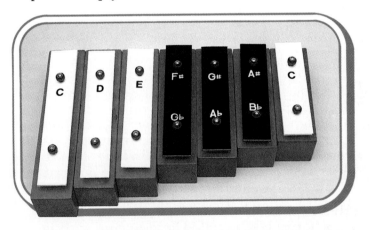

On the staff the pattern looks like this.

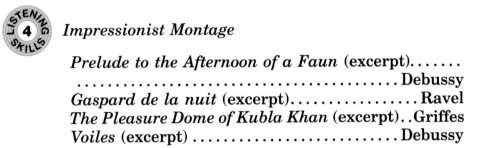

Play the pattern up and down. Then listen to the recording of the song "Silent Sea," on page 70. It is based entirely on a whole-tone scale. What effect does this have? Try playing the whole-tone scale after a major or minor scale. What do you hear that is different? Try singing "Silent Sea" to get the feel of the whole-tone scale.

Silent Sea

Words and Music by David Eddleman

Si - lent sea,   whis - per - ing;   With the warm wind

soft - ly sing.   Moon bath - ing in the   wa - ter,   gull wing   rest - ing.

Sea   will be   ver - y soon   sleep - ing in the   eye   of the   moon.

Claude Debussy's best-known composition may well be *Clair de lune*.
In this piano work Debussy attempted to capture in music the
moon's clear, cold light in warm, lush tones. This piano piece has
probably been played by everyone who ever studied piano for more
than a few years. Perhaps you have played it, too! Try writing down
descriptive words that occur to you as you listen.

Clair de lune . . . . Debussy

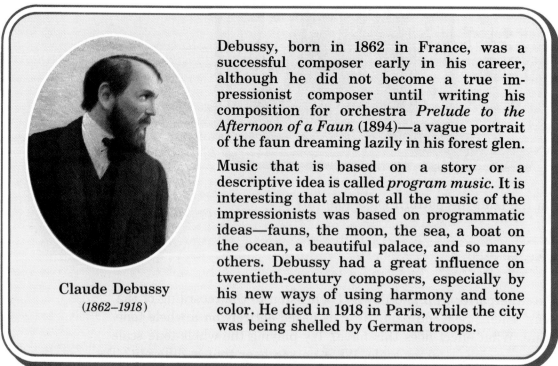

Claude Debussy
(1862–1918)

Debussy, born in 1862 in France, was a
successful composer early in his career,
although he did not become a true impressionist composer until writing his
composition for orchestra *Prelude to the
Afternoon of a Faun* (1894)—a vague portrait
of the faun dreaming lazily in his forest glen.

Music that is based on a story or a
descriptive idea is called *program music*. It is
interesting that almost all the music of the
impressionists was based on programmatic
ideas—fauns, the moon, the sea, a boat on
the ocean, a beautiful palace, and so many
others. Debussy had a great influence on
twentieth-century composers, especially by
his new ways of using harmony and tone
color. He died in 1918 in Paris, while the city
was being shelled by German troops.

The Twelve-Tone System

Play this scale pattern up and down to hear its special sound.

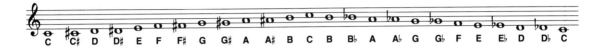

This scale is called a *chromatic scale*. There are *no* whole steps—only half steps. What kind of feel does this give to the sound?

Some composers in the twentieth century, led by a musician named Arnold Schoenberg (SHUHRN behrg), wrote music by arranging the twelve notes of the chromatic scale in a *tone row,* such as this.

Arrange your bells to fit the pattern above. Play the bells in order, to hear the special sound of the row. Now play the bells *backward* to hear that sound. The row can even be played upside down. It looks like this on the staff.

And this, too, can be played backward.

A twelve-tone composer would use *only* these forms of the row to construct a piece, and each note would have to be sounded before the next note could be heard.

The rows above are the rows Schoenberg used to write his *String Quartet No. 4.* By adding rhythms to the row, he could write melodies. Often, several notes will sound together as a chord. As you listen to the first movement, can you hear any of the tone rows? Don't be concerned if you can't. It's the total effect that is important.

String Quartet No. 4, Movement 1
(excerpt) . . . . Schoenberg

The Revolt of Rhythm

Clap this rhythm over and over.

$\begin{smallmatrix}4\\4\end{smallmatrix}$ ♩ ♩ ♩. ♪ |

And this one.

$\begin{smallmatrix}3\\4\end{smallmatrix}$ ♩. ♪♩ |

Over and over and over and over, the meter goes marching along. In the Renaissance, music flowed freely from meter to meter (as in "My Joy Would Grow in Measure"). Later, composers established the meter at the beginning of a piece and, with rare exceptions, that meter did not change throughout the piece. By the twentieth century, many composers were rebelling against what they called the "tyranny of the bar line." The Russian-born Igor Stravinsky, who is hailed by many as the composer whose music most typifies the twentieth century, hit upon a rhythmic independence that took him totally away from nineteenth-century Romantic style. Many feel that his ballet *The Rite of Spring* was the piece that truly brought music into the twentieth century.

The Rite of Spring

When *The Rite of Spring* was first performed in Paris in 1913, it created a scandal! The story was not about beautiful flowers and pleasant weather, the kind of fare that might be expected in a ballet with "spring" in its title. Instead, Stravinsky's music depicted primitive and savage ceremonies in Stone-Age Russia. There was frenzied dancing by people clothed in animal skins as they greeted the "rebirth" of the earth. At the end a young girl was sacrificed to appease the gods of spring.

Many in the audience that first night were scandalized by the story. Many felt it to be immoral and indecent. Something about the strong and insistent rhythms and the harsh dissonances provoked a negative response in them. People laughed and made catcalls. One journalist wrote that fights broke out, and he gradually became aware that the man in back of him was beating him over the head in rhythm! The journalist said that his emotion was so great he was unaware of the blows for some time!

There is no doubt that this music has great power both to attract and repel. Even now, some people may still be seen walking out of a performance of *The Rite of Spring,* protesting its dissonances and strong, erratic rhythms.

As you listen to the first section of *The Rite of Spring,* you will feel the unsteady, changing rhythms of Stravinsky's beginning. Try to feel the meter. It won't be easy! That is because the meter changes so rapidly; $\frac{4}{4}$, $\frac{3}{4}$, and $\frac{2}{4}$ go by very quickly, sometimes changing as often as every measure. You should be able to tell easily when the second section, "Dance of the Youths and Maidens," begins. The meter in this section is more consistent; it is $\frac{2}{4}$ most of the way. The rhythm is very emphatic and highly accented. To get a feel for the rhythm of "Dance of the Youths and Maidens," work out this rhythm score. You may clap the rhythms or use different classroom instruments.

 The Rite of Spring, "Introduction" and "Dance of the Youths and Maidens" (excerpt) .... Stravinsky

American Music Takes Its Place

Russian Easter Overture, Marche Slav, The Moldau, Hungarian Rhapsody—all these works from the nineteenth century celebrated *nationalism,* a movement that was reaching its height in Europe at that time. And in America, most composers were trying their best to sound just like their counterparts in Europe, especially those in Germany.

In the twentieth century, however, American composers—even those who had gone to Europe to study—became fascinated with the folk music of their own country. It was not enough for them to write symphonies and concertos and operas that sounded like the works of Brahms or Tchaikovsky. Composers Aaron Copland (KOH pluhnd), Virgil Thomson, Roy Harris, and others created works that captured the feel of America. They used not only folk music but folk*like* music that suggested the American rural scene. Copland's use of the open fifth (two notes that are five notes apart) suggested the great expanses of the American West. Listen to his *Fanfare for the Common Man* to discover how these open intervals seem to describe the vast frontier encountered by the pioneers.

Fanfare for the Common Man . . . . Copland

An Old Shaker Hymn Becomes a Suite

Aaron Copland has been called "the dean of American composers." Born in 1900, he has been a true child of the twentieth century. His love of American folk music has led him to produce many works that are uniquely American in sound and style.

You have probably sung the old Shaker hymn, "Simple Gifts." You will find it on page 325. Sing it and then listen to Copland's variations on this hymn in a suite from his ballet *Appalachian Spring*.

Call Chart 6

LISTENING SKILLS 5 Suite from *Appalachian Spring* . . . . Copland

1 "Simple Gifts" melody in clarinet; soft; thin accompaniment, short transition to Variation 1.

2 Variation 1: Melody
   Short transition to Variation 2

3 Variation 2: Long smooth tones
   Counterpoint
   Accompaniment, then short transition to Variation 3

4 Variation 3: Crescendo fanfare
   Instrument counterpoint; ff > > > >

5 Variation 4: Counterpoint
   mp
   Low tones accompanied

6 Variation 5: ff, slower; long tones, heavy accent; thick, full orchestra; strong final cadence

Music from Electronic Sources

Soon after World War II and the development of the tape recorder, many composers tried creating new sounds and new ways of putting sounds together. By manipulating the tape and by splicing tape in clever ways, American composer Otto Luening (LEW ning) was able to create a fresh new piece called *Fantasy in Space*. The instrument on the tape is a flute, but no flute could ever be played naturally the way it is played here!

 5 *Fantasy in Space* ....Luening

The Synthesizer

Every period has produced new instruments especially associated with it—the harpsichord in the Baroque period and the piano in the Romantic period, for example. Today we have a purely twentieth-century instrument—the electronic synthesizer.

At first the synthesizer was used only by a small group of trained musicians trying to find new ways to express themselves with music. Little by little, however, it has become a standard instrument—along with the electric guitar—in nearly every rock band. Its surprising ability to imitate as well as to create new sounds makes it a favorite among these musicians.

Listen to this synthesizer piece. Remember, most sounds in it were made electronically.

5 *L'Daddy*....................................Paich

The Minimalists

After decades of extreme complexity in music, some composers, especially those from a rock background, have tried to simplify their music by using the fewest of means. Listen to "Lighting the Torch" from *The Olympian*. Philip Glass wrote this music to open the 1984 Olympics. What do you hear in this piece? Do the melodies and harmonies change often or repeat?

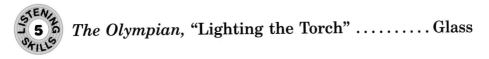

The Olympian, "Lighting the Torch" . . . . Glass

Did you hear all the parts being played over and over again? This repetition of simple melodies, rhythms, and harmonies has been called *minimalism*—reducing the musical elements to the minimal—the least.

Terry Riley has written a piece called *In C*. It is a kind of round in which 52 musical ideas are played in sequence. The players, however, play each idea as many times as they wish before going to the next one, and they may rest as long as they like between ideas. A piano provides unity by playing octave C's together high in the register. Listen to part of *In C*.

In C (excerpt). . . . . Riley

Try this musical exercise. It works something like Riley's *In C*. Players enter in sequence and play each idea over and over as long as they like before going to the next idea. They can rest between ideas for as long as they like (but don't take too long!). The piece is over when everyone has played the last idea. Try using a bell on C to play eighth notes throughout the exercise.

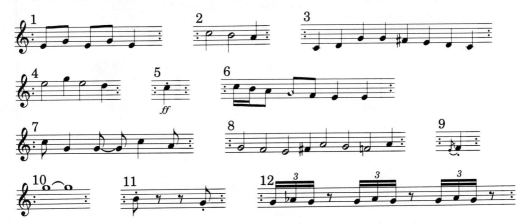

⑤

Now that you have heard a few pieces in different moods, listen to these selections. As you listen, circle the word that most closely describes the music. Use a blackline master or write the word on a separate sheet of paper.

Title	Mood	Tempo	Dynamics
1 *Fire Bell Polka* (excerpt)........Strauss	Festive Noble	Fast Moderate Slow	f p pp
2 *A German Requiem,* "How Lovely Is Thy Dwelling Place" (excerpt) .... Brahms	Light Dramatic	Fast Slow	f mf mp
3 *Aida,* "Grand March" (excerpt)..........Verdi	Noble Light	Moderate Slow	f pp
4 *Pictures at an Exhibition,* "Ballet of the Unhatched Chicks"......Mussorgsky	Humorous Dramatic	Fast Slow	mf p
5 *The Pines of Rome,* "Catacombs" (excerpt).... ....Respighi	Desolate Light	Fast Slow	f p
6 *Les Préludes* (excerpt).... ....Liszt	Noble Humorous	Fast Slow	f p

Test 1 ✓

The Renaissance

1. Two automobiles can have basically the same shape, but look different because they are in different _____.
   a. styles　　　　　b. showrooms　　　　　c. parking lots

2. Marches can be in different styles. Name three marches in different styles that you have heard.

   a. _____

   b. _____

   c. _____

3. Which of these instruments are *not* Renaissance period instruments? _____
   a. sackbut　　　　　b. recorder　　　　　c. krummhorn
   d. synthesizer　　　e. chalumeau　　　　f. piano

4. What does the word "Renaissance" mean? _____

5. A *catch* is a kind of _____.
   a. round　　　　　b. march　　　　　c. style

6. In the Renaissance, meters often alternated between meter in 2 and meter in 3. True or false? Circle your answer.
   a. True　　　　　b. False

7. During the Renaissance, composers often wrote music that sounded like something extramusical—birds, battles, and so forth. This technique is called _____.
   a. imitation　　　　b. word painting　　　　c. elements

8. *Polyphony* is a word that means _____.
   a. many melodic voices　　　　b. one melodic voice

9. In the Renaissance, musicians who traveled from town to town singing songs about the current events of the day were called _____.
   a. messengers　　　　b. conductors　　　　c. minstrels

10. A lively Renaissance dance was known as the _____.
    a. funky chicken　　　　b. bransle　　　　c. charleston

Test 2 ✓

The Baroque

1. One of the new instruments to be developed in the Baroque was the _____.
   a. recorder   b. violin   c. synthesizer

2. Vivaldi wrote many orchestra pieces for _____.
   a. strings only   b. flutes only   c. harpsichords only

3. In the "Autumn" concerto, third movement, of *The Four Seasons*, Vivaldi imitates the sounds of a hunt. This technique is called _____.
   a. trilling   b. hunting   c. tone painting

4. A new vocal form was developed during the Baroque. It was the *oratorio*. A great oratorio by Handel is _____.
   a. *The Four Seasons*   b. *Hallelujah*   c. *Messiah*

5. One of these composers is *not* a Baroque composer. Who is it?_____
   a. Bach   b. Vivaldi   c. Palestrina   d. Handel

6. An instrument that looks like a piano is the _____.
   a. flute   b. harpsichord   c. clarinet   d. cello

7. One instrument that was important in both the Renaissance and the Baroque periods was the _____.
   a. recorder   b. synthesizer   c. violin

8. The Baroque round "Where There Is Gladness" was written by _____.
   a. Stravinsky   b. Tourdion   c. Hayes   d. Sopranino

9. The Baroque period began about _____
   a. 1066   b. 1600   c. 1492
   and concluded around _____.
   d. 1936   e. 1750   f. 1865

10. During the Baroque, composers developed a melody-against-melody style that was a kind of _____.
    a. harmony   b. form   c. song   d. polyphony

The Classic Period

1. A good word to describe the term *classic* is _____.
   a. old   b. equality   c. painting

2. A *canon* is like a _____.
   a. song   b. concerto   c. round

3. The composer Salieri had a long rivalry with another Classic
   period composer. That composer's name was _____.
   a. Bach   b. Mozart   c. Sibelius   d. Rimsky-Korsakov

4. Composers during the Classic period began to use
   instruments that Baroque composers had not used. Among
   them was the _____.
   a. violin   b. piano   c. saxophone   d. recorder

5. A sense of balance and equality was a mark of the Classic
   period. As a result, composers gave new attention to _____.
   a. horns   b. tone painting   c. music   d. form

6. You listened to a Call Chart on a famous overture by
   Mozart. It was the overture to _____.
   a. *Swan Lake*   b. *Pictures at an Exhibition*
   c. *The Marriage of Figaro*   d. *Star Wars*

7. The classic round, or canon, is much like the Baroque _____.
   a. flute   b. catch   c. oratorio

8. Classic composers often wrote melodies supported by chords.
   This kind of texture is called _____.
   a. homophonic   b. monophonic   c. polyphonic

9. Music in the Baroque period was often very complex and
   polyphonic, whereas music in the Classic period seemed to
   have more _____.
   a. treble clefs   b. simplicity   c. scales

10. In the Baroque period, harmonies often changed on every
   beat. In the Classic period, the harmonies changed _____.
   a. on the beat   b. off the beat
   c. often only once or twice per measure

Test 4 ✓

The Romantic Period and Impressionism

1. One of the following was a novel of the Romantic period. Which one is it? _____
   a. *Dracula*   b. *The Four Seasons*   c. *The Hardy Boys*

2. One of the following is *not* associated with the Romantic period. Which one is it? _____
   a. large orchestras   b. love of nature
   c. ghosts   d. krummhorns

3. *Danse macabre,* by Camille Saint-Saëns, is a piece of descriptive music about _____.
   a. a storm at sea   b. a ghost fiddler   c. a horse race

4. In *Danse macabre,* the solo violinist is asked to tune the violin "out-of-tune." This makes it sound _____.
   a. loud   b. high   c. "spooky"   d. dark

5. Impressionism took its name from a painting called *Impression: Sunrise,* by the French painter _____.
   a. Kandinsky   b. Poulenc   c. Monet   d. Corot

6. In Impressionism the images are _____,
   a. vague   b. clear
   and the colors are _____.
   c. bright   d. muted

7. The best-known composer in impressionistic music was _____.
   a. Stravinsky   b. Gershwin   c. Riley
   d. Vivaldi   e. Debussy

8. Both *Danse macabre* and *Clair de lune* are examples of _____.
   a. solos   b. string pieces   c. program music

9. Debussy sometimes wrote his music on a distinctive scale known as the _____.
   a. major scale   b. minor scale   c. whole-tone scale

10. One of Debussy's most famous compositions is a piece called _____.
    a. *Danse macabre*   b. *Flight of the Bumblebee*
    c. *The Swan of Tuonela*   d. *Clair de lune*

Test 5 ✓

The Twentieth Century

1. Arnold Schoenberg invented a system of composition that used the _____.
   a. major row   b. twelve-tone row   c. minor row

2. In this system, Schoenberg used all the tones in the _____.
   a. whole-tone scale   b. minor scale
   c. chromatic scale

3. Many twentieth-century composers rebelled at the even $\frac{2}{4}$, $\frac{3}{4}$, and $\frac{4}{4}$ meters. They called it the _____.
   a. tyranny of the meter signature
   b. tyranny of the rhythms
   c. tyranny of the bar line

4. Igor Stravinsky wrote a ballet score that tried to be free of regular meter. It is called _____.
   a. *Prelude to the Afternoon of a Faun*
   b. *Grand Canyon Suite*
   c. *The Rite of Spring*

5. Aaron Copland arranged a suite from his ballet score, *Appalachian Spring*. It was a form called _____.
   a. variations   b. sonata   c. symphony   d. waltz

6. One of these instruments is associated only with the twentieth century. Which one is it? _____
   a. recorder   b. synthesizer   c. trumpet   d. krummhorn

7. A jazz-rock piece performed with synthesizer, *L'Daddy,* was composed by a twentieth-century composer named _____.
   a. Grofé   b. Williams   c. Sondheim   d. Paich

8. The minimalist movement has tried to make its music _____.
   a. more complex   b. simpler

9. *The Olympian* is an important score by the minimalist composer _____.
   a. Philip Glass   b. Terry Riley   c. Laura Dean

10. Terry Riley wrote a minimalist piece called _____.
    a. *The Nutcracker Suite*
    b. *Pomp and Circumstance*
    c. *In C*
    d. *Danse Macabre*

UNDERSTANDING MUSIC

Patterns into Form

Listen to this song before you sing it. Follow the two melodic
instrumental parts. Do you hear anything that repeats over and
over? Do you hear a rhythm that repeats? A melody that repeats? Is
anything repeated in the other two parts?

Rosie 5

Words and Music by Lawrence Eisman

ne - ver find _ her, I know; No, _ I'll ne - ver find _ her, I'll

ne - ver find _ her, I know. _____

last time, fade to end

"Rosie" has several short musical ideas that repeat over and over. A musical idea, whether melodic or rhythmic, that repeats over and over is called an *ostinato* (ah stee NAH toh). That's an Italian word that means "obstinate." Have you ever known people who acted in an obstinate way? Most of us have! They were headstrong and stubborn and wouldn't give up. The ostinato is like that. It goes on and on, refusing to let up and forcing the music around it to adjust to it. Being obstinate isn't always bad, especially if you're an ostinato!

Ostinato Patterns

Ostinatos may consist only of rhythms—that is, patterns of sounds without pitch—or of pitch and rhythm. Try playing each ostinato below on a different rhythm instrument. Divide your class into three groups and play them all together.

Ostinatos Together

The *blues* is perhaps the oldest form of jazz. In "Automotive Blues" you will hear four ostinatos above the bass part. Can you find them in the score?

Automotive Blues ⑤

Lawrence Eisman

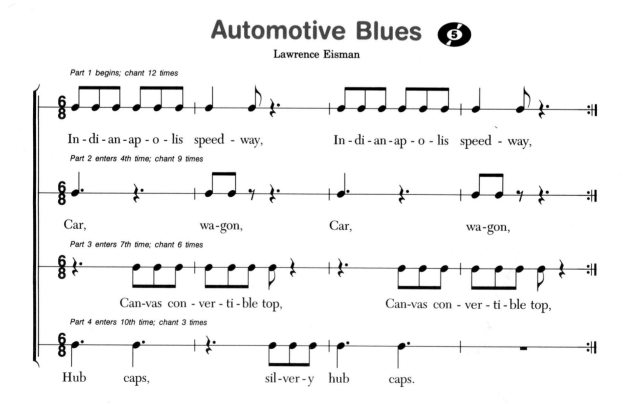

Part 1 begins; chant 12 times

In - di - an - ap - o - lis speed - way,

Part 2 enters 4th time; chant 9 times

Car, wa - gon,

Part 3 enters 7th time; chant 6 times

Can - vas con - ver - ti - ble top,

Part 4 enters 10th time; chant 3 times

Hub caps, sil - ver - y hub caps.

Ostinatos and Jazz

Do you know what a *riff* is? In jazz, an ostinato is often called a riff. Sometimes jazz musicians will have several riffs going together, as in "Automotive Blues."

In *Bellavia,* a composition about his mother, jazz musician Chuck Mangione uses an ostinato to unify his music. This is the ostinato he uses.

Mangione uses the ostinato in a number of ways. It doesn't always stay the same. Sometimes he varies it! Follow the Call Chart to see how the ostinato is used to create both unity and variety in *Bellavia.*

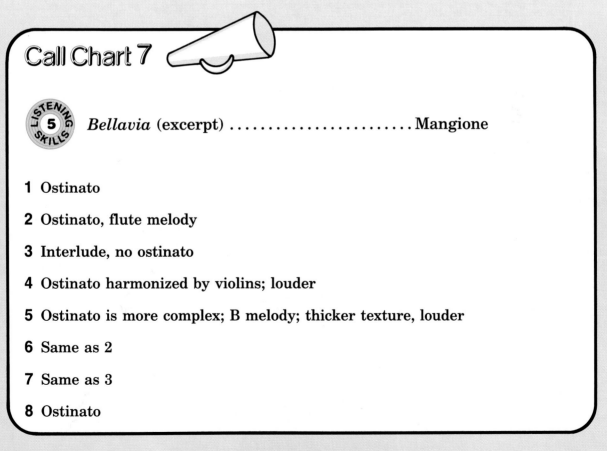

Call Chart 7

(5) LISTENING SKILLS *Bellavia* (excerpt) .... Mangione

1 Ostinato

2 Ostinato, flute melody

3 Interlude, no ostinato

4 Ostinato harmonized by violins; louder

5 Ostinato is more complex; B melody; thicker texture, louder

6 Same as 2

7 Same as 3

8 Ostinato

Jazzin' Ostinatos (or SING THAT RIFF!)

Few things are as much fun for musicians as performing a group of riffs. Jazz singers do this as well. And when several get together and perform riffs, it can be very exciting. Here is a set of riffs written especially for you. The top part has one riff, the bottom part another, and the bass instrument adds still another. The parts are all written together, but notice that all don't come in at the same time. First, the bass starts. (It can be played on piano; it is also on a special track on the recording. Or perhaps a class member who plays a bass can perform this part.) After the bass plays the riff once through, the bottom part enters with its riff, then the top part joins in. Finally, everyone performs the riffs together, and the piece finishes. Can you think of a good way to finish? Perhaps shaking your hands in the air in good old jazz style!

Riff-le Along

Words and Music by David Eddleman

Let's Hear It for the Ostinatos

You can hear ostinatos used in most styles of music. Some ostinatos may be only rhythm patterns, and others will be melodic as well as rhythmic. Listen to each example. The notation shows you the ostinato. Listen for it and tell how or where it is used.

You may think it's sneaky, but one of the examples notated below is *not* an ostinato. Can you tell which one it is?

5 *Ostinato Examples*

1. *Bellavia* . . . . Mangione

2. *Hear the Bell* . . . . Eddleman

3. *Jaguar* . . . . Benson

4. *Eine kleine Nachtmusik*, Movement 1 . . . . Mozart

5. *Esther*, "Thro' the Nation" . . . . Handel

6. *Concerto in G Minor for Strings* . . . . Vivaldi

By now you must realize that a main purpose of the ostinato is to provide unity. Look at this ostinato.

Hear the bell, hear it toll.

Easy, isn't it? Now play or sing the ostinato as others sing the round "Hear the Bell." You might start the ostinato first as an introduction.

Hear the Bell ⑤

Words and Music by David Eddleman

Hear the bell toll - ing; the an - cient chime __ is whis - per - ing ___ for

me: ___ "Come to my king - dom un - der the sea." ___

As short as it is, "Hear the Bell" has both unity and variety. The ostinato helps to provide unity, and the melody provides variety.

Variation within unity can be found almost everywhere. For example, look at your classmates. You have heads, bodies, arms, legs, and so forth. That's the unity. But some have blond hair, some have black, brown, or red hair; some are tall, others are short. Some have blue eyes, others have brown or green or hazel eyes. That's the variety.

Making Friends

When you meet someone for the first time, how do you react? You probably are interested in knowing what the person is like. You want to get to know the "new kid on the block" to see if he or she will make a good friend.

In order to do this, you observe the person carefully. You listen to what the person has to say. As you become aware of the person's personality, you begin to learn about your new friend. He or she begins to "make sense."

A piece of music can be like your new friend. You need to listen to it carefully to understand it. This is true whether the piece of music is a symphony, a folk song, or the hottest new rock release.

Here is a piece of music by Handel. Do you remember it? This piece is based on an ostinato.

How much can you learn about the piece just by listening to it? You can use these questions to focus your attention.

Esther, "Thro' the Nations He Shall Be".....Handel

1. What instruments play the ostinato?
2. Does the ostinato have
   • Mostly long sounds or mostly short sounds?
   • Steps or wide leaps?
   • Meter in 2 or 3?
3. How many measures does the ostinato contain?
4. How much of the ostinato can you perform? Clap?
5. Can you perform any smaller patterns within the ostinato?

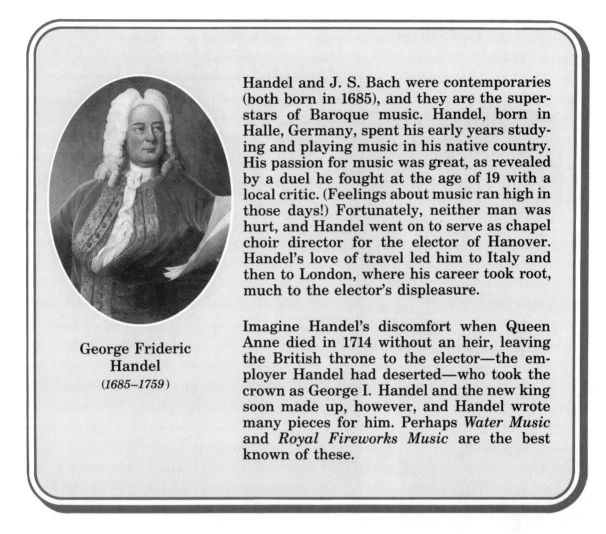

Handel and J. S. Bach were contemporaries (both born in 1685), and they are the superstars of Baroque music. Handel, born in Halle, Germany, spent his early years studying and playing music in his native country. His passion for music was great, as revealed by a duel he fought at the age of 19 with a local critic. (Feelings about music ran high in those days!) Fortunately, neither man was hurt, and Handel went on to serve as chapel choir director for the elector of Hanover. Handel's love of travel led him to Italy and then to London, where his career took root, much to the elector's displeasure.

Imagine Handel's discomfort when Queen Anne died in 1714 without an heir, leaving the British throne to the elector—the employer Handel had deserted—who took the crown as George I. Handel and the new king soon made up, however, and Handel wrote many pieces for him. Perhaps *Water Music* and *Royal Fireworks Music* are the best known of these.

George Frideric
Handel
(1685–1759)

Handel in England

Handel had gone to England to get involved with the country's craze for Italian opera. He became well-known as a composer of Italian opera, and made a fortune in England exploiting this talent.

When the British grew tired of opera Handel turned to writing oratorios. These were epic or religious music dramas with characters and plot, but without scenery or costumes. They called for chorus, soloists, and full orchestra, and were often sung in English.

He turned out one successful oratorio after another—*Judas Maccabaeus, Jephtha, Samson, Deborah, Israel in Egypt*. But his most famous oratorio is one that has only a loose plot—*Messiah*. You heard the "Hallelujah" chorus from *Messiah* on page 45.

Music Is a Thing of Parts

Jigsaw Your Way to a Jazz-Rock Piece

Archaeologists uncover an ancient city—perhaps Babylon, Megiddo, Ur, Nineveh, or, as on page 96, Tenochtitlán (teh nohch teet LAHN, now Mexico City). As they dig, they find buildings and artifacts thousands of years old, wonderfully preserved during the slow press of time by their covering of earth as they could not have been in the open. Archaeologists can reconstruct whole civilizations by examining the bits and pieces that remain.

Working like archaeologists, let's build a whole musical piece—one you may know—from its separate parts. Here are our own musical "bits and pieces."

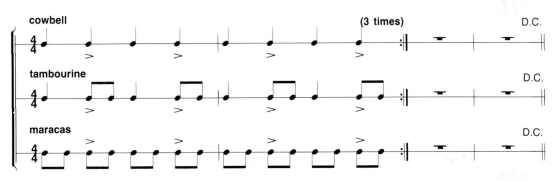

Add this two-part melodic pattern on bells or other melody instruments. It has the same rhythm as the tambourine part.

Now add the autoharp, string bass, or electric bass.

Finally, add a piano.

And This Is What It Becomes

If you know your jazz-rock classics, you will already have recognized the accompaniment to "Spinning Wheel." As the rock group Blood, Sweat and Tears sings "Spinning Wheel," listen to the way the patterns on page 97 are used to create the sections of the song. Some patterns are the same, some are similar, and others are completely different.

Spinning Wheel 6

Words and Music by David Clayton-Thomas

What goes_ up   must come_ down,   Spin-nin' wheel

got to go 'round._   Talk-in' 'bout your trou-bles, it's a   cry-in' sin, _

Ride   a   paint-ed   po-ny,   let   the   spin-nin'   wheel_   spin.

Ya got no mon-ey, and ya, ya got no home,_____ Spin-nin' wheel

all a - lone,_ Talk-in' 'bout your trou-bles and ya, ya nev-er learn,_

Ride a paint-ed po - ny, let the spin-nin' wheel _ turn.

Did you find _ a di - rect-ing sign _ on the straight and _ nar - row

high - way? _ Would you mind _ a re - flect-ing sign? _ Just

let it shine _ with - in your mind _ and show you _ the

co - lors _____ that are real. _____ Some-one is wait - in'

just for you, _____ Spin-nin' wheel spin-nin' true. _____

Drop all your trou - bles by the riv - er - side, _

Catch a paint-ed po - ny on the spin-nin' wheel _ ride.

Filling Out Forms

What do you notice about the pictures below? Each picture consists of two like subjects separated by an unlike subject. If we call the like subjects A and the unlike subjects B, then each group can be labeled ABA. Sections of music, too, are like and unlike. ABA is one of the most common musical forms.

Many songs repeat the first A section, making the form actually AABA. The principle of the form is still the same, however—two like sections separated by an unlike section.

Here is a song in ABA form. The sections are clearly labeled. After you have sung the song, try to think of other songs that are in ABA form.

Little David, Play on Your Harp

Black Spiritual

Listen to this composition. As you listen, look at the form patterns below. Can you tell which pattern best shows the form of the music?

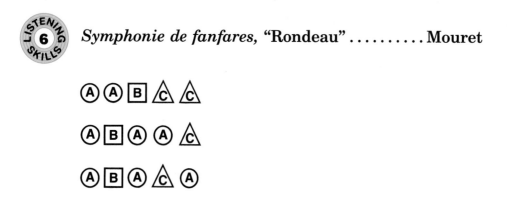

LISTENING SKILLS 6

Symphonie de fanfares, "Rondeau" . . . . Mouret

This piece by Campra is in the same form as the Mouret piece.

LISTENING SKILLS 6

Tancredi, "Triumphal March" . . . . Campra

The Mouret and Campra pieces are both rondos. (The title of Mouret's piece uses the French spelling, but it's pronounced the same as the Italian word *rondo*.) A rondo has this form.

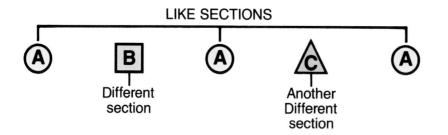

LIKE SECTIONS

(A)   **B**   (A)   △C   (A)

Different section   Another Different section

No matter how many different sections appear in a rondo, section A always separates them, returning over and over and over until it concludes the rondo with a final appearance.

Here is a song in rondo form. You will see that the sections are clearly marked.

How Good the Time

(Hineh Mah Tov)

Traditional Hebrew Words   Music by A. Jacobson   English Words by Alexander Hirsch

Underneath the Arches

As you listen to this piece by a modern composer, jot down the letter name for each section on a separate sheet of paper. Don't write the letter twice if a section is repeated immediately.

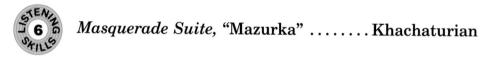 *Masquerade Suite, "Mazurka"* .... **Khachaturian**

If you listened carefully, you found that the form of "Mazurka" is ABCBA. This form—retreating from and returning to A—is called an *arch* form.

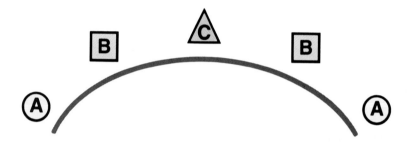

An Arch with a Twist

Here is an arch form with something a little different at the end. Listen for it.

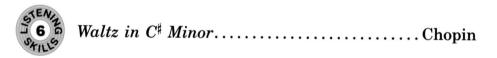 *Waltz in C♯ Minor* .... **Chopin**

Did you follow the form? What made this different from other arch forms? Right! The B section showed up again at the end. This is the form in diagram.

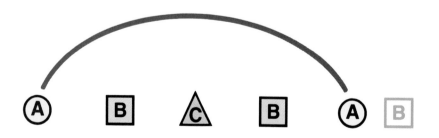

Repetition and Variety

What do you see that repeats in these pictures? All the houses are basically alike. How about the potatoes? Yes, they're all potatoes.

What things are different? The houses are different colors, and the potatoes are prepared in different ways—potato salad, a baked potato, potato soup, and a potato casserole.

Repetition and variety—these are two very important elements in making sure music is interesting and fun to listen to. In this recording, Blood, Sweat, and Tears use repetition and variety by stating a melodic theme and following it with four variations. Can you hear them?

Variations on a Theme by Erik Satie . . . .
. . . . Blood, Sweat, and Tears

American Salute

When Johnny Comes Marching Home

Words and Music by Patrick Gilmore

1. When John-ny comes march-ing home a-gain, Hur-rah!___ Hur-rah!___ We'll
2. Get read-y for the ju-bi-lee, Hur-rah!___ Hur-rah!___ We'll

give him a heart-y wel-come then, Hur-rah!___ Hur-rah!___ The ___
give___ the he-ro three times three, Hur-rah!___ Hur-rah!___ The ___

men will cheer_ the boys will shout, The la-dies they_ will all turn out, And we'll
lau-rel wreath_ is read-y now To place up-on___ his loy-al brow, And we'll

shout "Hoo - ray!" when John-ny comes march-ing home!___
shout "Hoo - ray!" when John-ny comes march-ing home!___

In his orchestral piece *American Salute*, Morton Gould uses "When Johnny Comes Marching Home" as the basis for a set of variations. Just as the houses and potatoes are still recognizable even though varied, so the melody of "When Johnny Comes Marching Home" is still recognizable, even in Gould's variations. Follow the Call Chart on page 107 to hear how he does it.

Call Chart 8

LISTENING SKILLS 6 *American Salute* . . . . Gould

1 INTRODUCTION: Based on rhythms from the song.

2 MELODY A: Bassoon and bass clarinet.
ACCOMPANIMENT: Violins and snare drum play rhythm pattern of the introduction.

3 BRIDGE: Violins and snare drums continue rhythm pattern. Muted brasses play this fragment:

4 MELODY A^1: English horn.
ACCOMPANIMENT: Low woodwinds.
VARIATION: Change in instrumentation.

5 MELODY A^2: Strings.
ACCOMPANIMENT: Brasses and woodwinds.
VARIATION: Change in instrumentation again.

6 BRIDGE: Brasses and timpani play rhythmic fragments.

7 MELODY A^3: High woodwinds.
VARIATION: Rhythmic and melodic variations; all notes of equal length.

8 BRIDGE: Woodwinds and strings play a crescendo.

9 MELODY A^4: Variation: Rhythm is syncopated; $\frac{4}{4}$

10 BRIDGE: Meter changes from $\frac{2}{2}$ to $\frac{4}{4}$

11 MELODY A^5: Variation in two parts.

PART I
MELODY: Trumpets and trombones.
VARIATION: Rhythmic variations; note values are lengthened, a device called *augmentation*.

12 PART II
MELODY: Woodwinds.
VARIATION: Rhythmic variation; $\frac{12}{8}$
CODA: Fragments of the theme; final statement with phrases separated by an interlude; accelerando.

Which Came First, the Chicken or the Egg?

Questions about which came first have been asked by people for many centuries. Of course, such questions cannot really be answered, but they serve to teach us that everything grows from something else. A flower, a stalk of corn, or a tree—like the oak above—all grow from seeds. And yes, an egg produces a chicken that, in turn, produces another egg! So it goes, a constant unfoldment.

Music, too, grows from small seeds. Sing this musical seed, something we call in music a *motive*.

G G E E

You probably recognized that as the motive for "America, the Beautiful." As you sing "America, the Beautiful," notice how the motive is varied. The motive and its variations are marked in your music.

America, the Beautiful 6

Music by Samuel A. Ward   Words by Katherine Lee Bates

3. O beautiful for heroes proved In liberating strife,
   Who more than self their country loved, And mercy more than life!
   America! America! May God thy gold refine,
   Till all success be nobleness, And ev'ry gain divine!

4. O beautiful for patriot dream That sees, beyond the years,
   Thine alabaster cities gleam Undimmed by human tears!
   America! America! God shed His grace on thee,
   And crown thy good with brotherhood, From sea to shining sea!

What's the Motive?

The intrepid Sherlock Holmes is at work again—joined by his sidekick, Dr. Watson—to solve another *Murder Most Foul* and *Render Justice* to the *Evil Perpetrator!* Read the script as Holmes, with *Impeccable Logic*, uncovers the motive for the *Dastardly Deed.*

THE SCENE: *A desolate moor in Yorkshire, England.*

SHERLOCK HOLMES: This stone may interest you, Lestrade. The murder was done with it.

INSPECTOR LESTRADE: I see no marks.

HOLMES: There are none.

DR. WATSON: How do you know then, Holmes?

HOLMES: The grass was growing under it, so it could only have been there a few days. And it corresponds with the injuries.

LESTRADE: And the criminal . . . ?

HOLMES: Is a tall man, left-handed, limps with the right leg, wears thick-soled shooting boots and a gray cloak, smokes Indian cigars, uses a cigar-holder, and carries a blunt penknife in his pocket.

WATSON: Astounding, Holmes. You never cease to amaze me! But what could have been the *motive* for such a crime?

HOLMES: Elementary, my dear Watson. The criminal needed a way out of England. That meant money he didn't have. But his brother's will specified he could inherit his estate only if he did not die by foul play. The stone made it appear that the victim had died accidentally! Therefore the criminal could inherit his brother's fortune! That was the *motive*. That is what *motivated* him to set the game afoot!

WATSON: Good heavens, Holmes. Then you've solved the crime?

HOLMES: Indeed, Watson, the murderer is . . .

Just as a detective, like the legendary Sherlock Holmes, must find a motive for criminal behavior—a reason that *motivates* a criminal's actions—so a composer or songwriter must find a motive that will motivate a complete song, symphony, or sonata. "Carolina in the Morning," page 155, and "I Want to Be Happy," page 134, both have motives you can recognize clearly.

Many good musicians can improvise an entire composition on a single motive. Look at this one. Sing it on *la*.

Dave Brubeck was shown that motive and asked to improvise on it. Can you follow the motive as he plays?

 Improvisation. . . . . **Brubeck**

Careers in Music—Performing

Dave Brubeck proved his improvisational skills on page 111. Both he and Wynton Marsalis are fine musicians with a strong background of academic training. Listen as they talk about their careers in performing and creating.

 Careers in Music—Dave Brubeck

 Second Improvisation
.... Brubeck

From Motive to Composition

How about composing your own piece to a motive? It really isn't too hard. Here's a pattern of chords with text underneath. There isn't any rhythm.

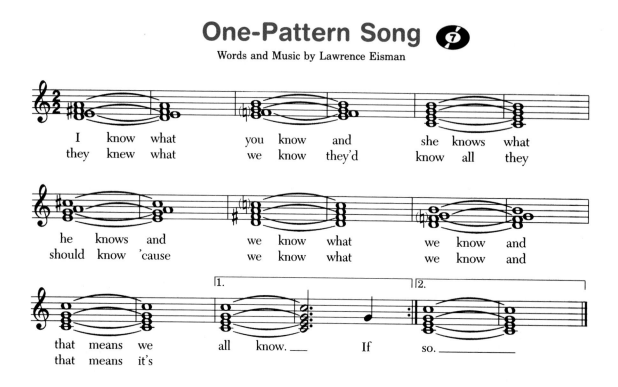

One-Pattern Song

Words and Music by Lawrence Eisman

I know what you know and she knows what
they knew what we know they'd know all they

he knows and we know what we know and
should know 'cause we know what we know and

that means we all know. ___ If so. ___
that means it's

Choose a chord tone for each two-measure phrase and sing it in this rhythmic motive:

For example, if the note you select for the first two measures is A, those measures would be:

I know ___ what

Don't use any large leaps. Stick to moving by step or by repeated tones. An occasional short leap, say from A to F or something similar, might be interesting.

Here is the chord pattern recorded for you to sing with. First chant the words in rhythm to the accompaniment. Then try singing on the notes you've chosen. The accompaniment follows this routine.

Introduction: 4 measures
Accompaniment: 16 measures
Instrumental interlude: 8 measures
Accompaniment: 16 measures
Coda: 4 measures

Chord-Pattern Accompaniment

Here is how composer Vincent Youmans, along with lyricist Anne Caldwell, crafted the rhythmic motive and the harmonies into a song.

I Know that You Know

Words by Anne Caldwell   Music by Vincent Youmans

Motive Builders

Have you studied molecules in your science classes? All that we see is built out of molecules—the building blocks of matter. Music is built of motives—the building blocks of music. Molecules themselves, of course, are made up of smaller units—atoms. Motives, too, can be made of smaller units. We call those atomlike units *cells*. Look at this rhythmic motive.

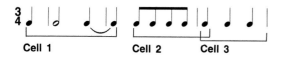

Can you see that the motive is made up of three cells? Try clapping the motive or playing it on a rhythm instrument. Then break it down and play each of the three cells. What do you notice about cells 2 and 3? If you said they overlap, you were right.

Here is the rhythmic pattern of the opening section of a minuet by Mozart. Try clapping it or playing it on a rhythm instrument.

What did you notice about this section? You were right if you saw that every measure consisted of one of the cells above. Mozart was able to construct an entire section of 14 measures just from the three cells in the motive.

Now listen to the minuet and follow the line score on page 117. What you have seen and clapped is the A section. You will hear a contrasting B section. Each section is repeated.

Minuet

Symphony No. 40 in G Minor, Movement 3,
"Minuet" . . . . Mozart

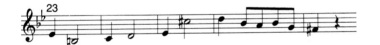

117

Pattern in a Pattern in a Pattern Makes a Pattern

What musical form do these three pictures remind you of?
That's right—the ABA form. But look closer. The pictures have patterns.
Patterns within patterns. The patterns can be compared to cells and
motives in music, which is built from cells to motives to sections
to forms. And forms can be expanded to make even larger forms.

Mozart's minuet is a very clear AB form. But that is not the whole
work. The minuet is followed by another AB section called the *trio*.
After the trio is played, the original minuet is repeated. That's ABA.
Audiences hearing a piece like this often try to listen for the formal
structure. Listen to the whole minuet and trio and follow the chart
to see how a large ABA form is built—from cells to motives to
sections to form.

Symphony No. 40 in G Minor, Movement 3,
"Minuet and Trio".................Mozart

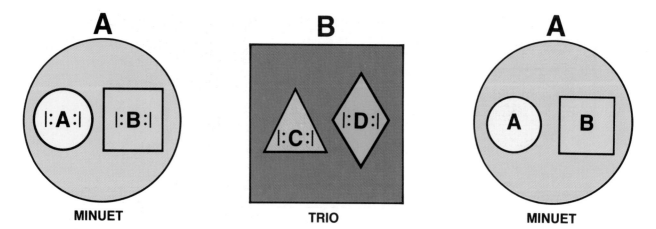

And Now for the Big One!

You may not know the name for it, but you probably have heard the musical form called *sonata-allegro*. Even some rock musicians have tried it! Sonata-allegro is a kind of overextended ABA with lots of variation and some sophisticated turns of melody, rhythm, and harmony.

The three sections of sonata-allegro have names. Let's introduce them.

EXPOSITION **DEVELOPMENT** **RECAPITULATION**

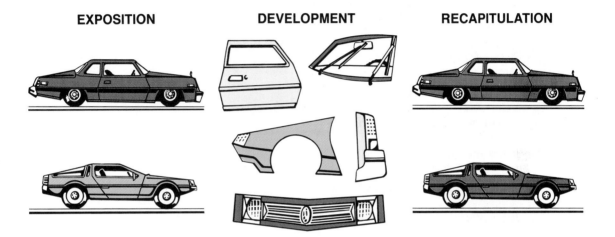

1. **EXPOSITION.** Usually two themes are introduced here. The first theme, theme 1, is ordinarily short and rhythmic and rather "muscular." The second theme, theme 2, most often contrasts with theme 1 by being gentler, more lyric, and sometimes softer. After the two themes are heard several times, a short coda, or ending, finishes the section.

2. **DEVELOPMENT.** Here the two themes are varied in many ways. Rhythms are changed; the melody may be changed by substituting different intervals; small cells and motives from the themes may be played at different pitch levels. The composer uses all his or her cleverness to wring every drop of variation out of the two themes. Sometimes the composer may develop one theme and ignore the other.

3. **RECAPITULATION.** Here we are back to our two cars. After all that variation, we need to hear those two themes again. And sure enough, the composer now gives them to us once more. Some composers will develop their themes a little more before the piece is over. Beethoven especially loved this trick. They sometimes even introduce a new theme! That's why it is important to listen carefully. You never know when the composer is going to surprise you! That's part of the magic of good music-making.

Call Chart 9

Here is a sonata-allegro form that was written in the eighteenth century. Follow the Call Chart to hear how the symphony works.

(7) LISTENING SKILLS *Symphony No. 40 in G Minor,* Movement 1 . . Mozart

EXPOSITION

1 ‖: Main theme

2 Main theme repeated; varied

3 New theme; contrast to main theme

4 Another new theme; contrasting

5 Ending of exposition; bits of the main theme used :‖

DEVELOPMENT

6 Main theme developed; changes in instruments, intervals, rhythms, direction, dynamics, texture

7 Bit of the main theme over and over, then

8 Ending of the development section; leads gradually to

RECAPITULATION

9 Main theme again

10 Main theme repeated; varied

11 New theme; contrast to main theme; extended to a strong cadence

12 Second new theme; contrasting

13 Ending of recapitulation section; bits of main theme used

14 CODA: ending section moves to a strong cadence

A Spoken Sonata-Allegro

You might think it is difficult to sing a sonata-allegro, but here is a
sonata-allegro that has only words and rhythms. It will give you an
idea of how the sonata-allegro works.

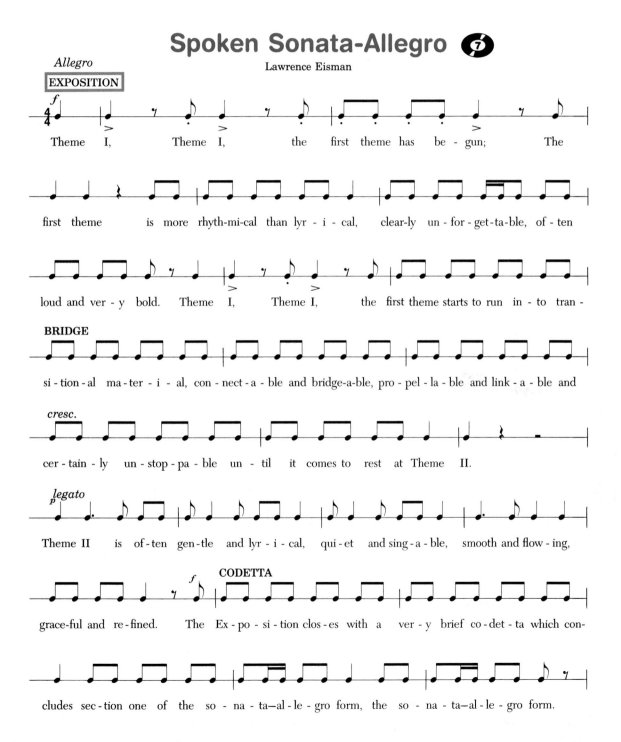

Spoken Sonata-Allegro

Lawrence Eisman

nect‑a‑ble and bridge‑a‑ble, pro‑pel‑la‑ble and link‑a‑ble and cer‑tain‑ly un‑stop‑pa‑ble un‑

p   *legato*

til it comes to rest at Theme II (soft‑er now).   Theme II   is of‑ten gen‑tle and lyr‑i‑cal,

f

qui‑et and sing‑a‑ble, smooth and flow‑ing, grace‑ful and re‑fined.   The

CODA

Re‑ca‑pit‑u‑la‑tion clos‑es off this ex‑plo‑ra‑tion with a sec‑tion called a Co‑da (in I‑

tal‑ian mean‑ing "tail"). It's con‑clud‑a‑ble ma‑ter‑i‑al drives rest‑less‑ly, re‑lent‑less‑ly,

cresc.

bring‑ing to an end the so‑na‑ta—al‑le‑gro form, the so‑

ff

na‑ta—al‑le‑gro form, so‑na‑ta—al‑le‑gro, so‑na‑ta‑al‑le‑gro form.

La Musica
by Giuseppe Zocchi

Test 6 ✓

The sentences below describe ostinatos. Write T if the statement is true or F if the statement is false.

1. An ostinato is a musical idea that repeats over and over.

   _____

2. *Ostinato* comes from an Italian word that means "flexible."

   _____

3. An ostinato must be repeated exactly the same way.

   _____

4. Ostinatos may consist only of rhythms, or of pitch and rhythm. _____

5. The most recent form of jazz is the *blues.* _____

6. In jazz, an ostinato is called a *riff.* _____

7. "Automotive Blues" consists of one riff. _____

8. In *Bellavia,* Chuck Mangione uses an ostinato in a number of ways. _____

9. A main purpose of the ostinato is to provide unity.

   _____

10. Ostinatos are used only in jazz and rock. _____

Test 7 ✓

Draw a line to connect the words on the right to the phrases that describe them.

1. J. S. Bach

2. London

3. *Judas Maccabeus*

4. oratorio

5. *Water Music*

6. Halle, Germany

7. *Messiah*

8. opera

9. King George I

10. "Hallelujah" Chorus

A. An oratorio by Handel with only a loose plot

B. The place where Handel's career took root

C. A contemporary of Handel's

D. Handel went to England to get involved with the country's craze for it

E. Handel's birthplace

F. A piece written for King George I

G. A successful oratorio of Handel's with a plot

H. Music drama with characters and plot, but without scenery and costumes

I. A famous chorus from Handel's *Messiah*

J. King of England who had been the elector of Hanover under whom Handel served

Test 8 ✓

Fill in the blanks with the correct word or words from the list below.

AABA	unlike section
rondo	B section
A section	ABACA
theme with variations	

1. In ABA form, two like sections are separated by an

_____ .

2. When the first section of an ABA song repeats immediately,

the form is labeled _____ .

3. No matter how many different sections appear in a

_____ , section A always separates them,
returning over and over again until it concludes it with a
final appearance.

4. An *arch* form retreats from A and returns to

_____ .

5. A A¹ A² A³ A⁴ is a label for this form: _____ .

6. Chopin's *Waltz in C# Minor* is an example of an arch form in

which the _____ shows up again at the end.

To answer the questions below, write T if the statement is true
and F if the statement is false.

7. ABA is called rondo form. _____

8. Sonata-allegro form is an extended ABA. _____

Test 9 ✓

The form of each song listed below is either AB, ABA or rondo form. Look through the music, and on your worksheet, write the name of the form in the blank. Use the song index in your book to find the page number of each song.

1. "Little David, Play on Your Harp" _____

2. "Cielito lindo" _____

3. "The Varsity Drag" _____

4. "How Good the Time" _____

Fill in the blanks with the correct word or words from the list below.

coda	recapitulation
trio	sonata-allegro
development	exposition

5. A more extended ABA form with lots of variation and some sophisticated turns of melody, rhythm, and harmony is

_____.

6. The middle section of the minuet-and-trio form is called the

_____.

7. The themes of a piece in sonata-allegro form are introduced in the _____.

8. The themes are varied in many different ways in the _____ of sonata-allegro form.

9. The section of sonata-allegro form in which the themes return and are concluded is called the _____.

10. A _____, or ending, finishes the exposition in sonata-allegro form.

PERFORMING MUSIC

CHAPTER 4—SINGING IN GROUPS

The phone rings. You pick up the receiver and say, "Hello?"

"Hi! What'll we do tomorrow after school?" asks a voice.

Without even thinking, you know it's your best friend. How did you know who it was? How did the person who was calling know from just the word *hello* that it was you on the other end of the line?

Everyone has a certain kind of voice quality and a particular way of saying words. Voice quality, just like fingerprints, is different in everyone.

Good Impressions

Some performers—like the impressionist Rich Little, pictured above with some of the familiar performers he imitates—can amaze you with their impersonations of famous people, but they cannot fool the machine that makes voice prints. There is something in each voice that has its own unique quality. Since the machine can detect even the smallest differences, it cannot be deceived.

Using your own voice, record a sentence into a cassette recorder. Change your voice as much as you can. Make it lower or higher than usual. Imitate a famous person, use the dialogue on page 111, and pretend you're an actor trying out for a part in a show.

Home in on Your Range

In the following recordings you will hear male voices singing in high and low registers. The high voices have a different voice quality from the soloist, who sings in a lower range.

 Getaway .... Taylor and Cor

Ol' Man River .... Kern and Hammerstein

Even if each singer sang at the same pitch, each voice would still have a distinctive voice quality. The same rules apply to your speaking voice as to your singing voice. Every voice has its own range—the lowest to the highest pitch the voice can sing.

Let's find *your* range. Find a comfortable pitch on the piano and sing it, using the syllable *dah* or *doo*. Now sing down the scale, using the white keys to help you. When you can go no lower without sounding raspy or breathy, you have reached the bottom of your range. Go back to your original pitch, and sing in an upward direction until you reach the highest pitch you can sing easily. That is the top of your range. Now, with the help of your teacher, make a chart of your total range. It might look like this:

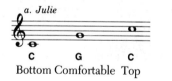

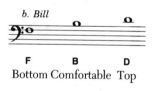

After you have drawn your range chart, compare it with your friends' charts. Some of their ranges may be higher or lower than your range. That is one reason why their voices sound different from your voice. Keep your range chart. Some time later, try again to see if you've added any pitches to the bottom or the top. If you have, add the new pitches to your range chart, using another color of ink.

Can You Find Your Part?

Example *d,* on page 131, shows that the singer, Bill, gained some pitches at the bottom but stayed the same at the top. This often happens to male singers at your age. It means that the voice is changing, getting lower, because the vocal cords are thickening and getting longer. Check your voice often. Keep adding, with different colors of ink or pencil, any new pitches you gain.

In "Climb Ev'ry Mountain," soprano, alto, tenor, and baritone sections are labeled. Which pitches are more like your range? Sing along on those sections only.

Climb Ev'ry Mountain

from *The Sound of Music*

Words by Oscar Hammerstein II   Music by Richard Rodgers
Arranged by Mary E. Hoffman

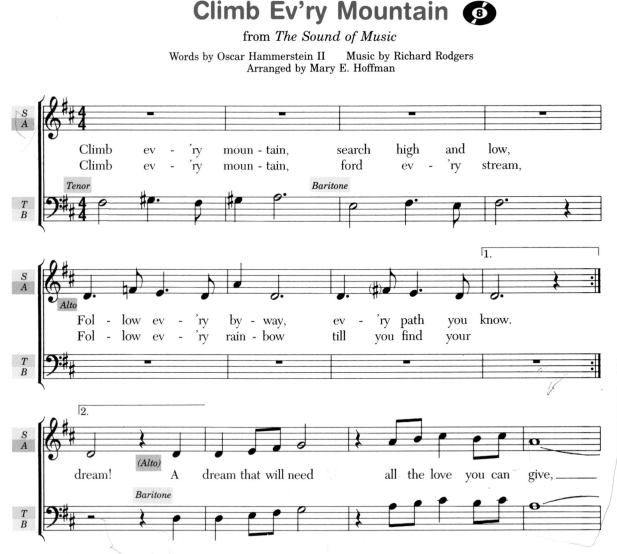

Climb ev - 'ry moun - tain, search high and low,
Climb ev - 'ry moun - tain, ford ev - 'ry stream,

Fol - low ev - 'ry by - way, ev - 'ry path you know.
Fol - low ev - 'ry rain - bow till you find your

dream! A dream that will need all the love you can give, ___

Ev - 'ry day of your life for as long as you live. _____

Slower

Climb ev - 'ry moun - tain, ford ev - 'ry

stream, Fol - low ev - 'ry rain - bow till you

find your dream! _____

In "I Want to Be Happy," there are two parts—one for sopranos and altos singing in unison and one for tenors and baritones singing in unison. This is possible because some notes in the soprano and alto, and tenor and baritone ranges overlap, and can be sung by either voice.

I Want to Be Happy

from *No, No, Nanette*

Words by Irving Caesar   Music by Vincent Youmans   Arranged by Mary E. Hoffman

Soprano, Alto

I want to be hap-py, but I won't be hap-py

Tenor, Baritone

I want to be hap-py, but I won't be hap-py

till I make you hap-py, too; _____ Life's real-ly

till I make you hap-py, so ver-y hap-py; Life's real-ly

worth liv-ing, when we are mirth-giv-ing, Why can't I

worth liv-ing, when we are mirth-giv-ing, Why can't I

Voices Singing Separately

In "This Guy's in Love with You," on page 136, the voices are in two parts again but sing basically the same melody when they sing together. The *score* is written just like the song on page 132, with a staff for the soprano and alto parts in the treble clef and a staff for the tenors and baritones in the bass clef. This kind of staff combination is called a *great,* or *grand staff.*

This Guy's in Love with You

Words by Hal David   Music by Burt Bacharach   Arranged by Mary E. Hoffman

A Change in the Voice

In a scene from the musical play *The Music Man* Harold Hill has taught a young boy, Winthrop, to sing "Gary, Indiana." Since Winthrop is a young boy, his voice has a high quality. But Harold Hill, the "Music Man," sounds much lower while singing his section. When Winthrop teaches the song to his mother and his sister Marian, *they* join him in singing.

Listen to these different voices—first Winthrop (the boy),

then Harold Hill (the man),

and then Marian

and her mother (the women).

 8 *Gary, Indiana*—voice segments

Now listen to the complete song. Can you tell when the boy is singing? The man? The women?

 8 *Gary, Indiana*

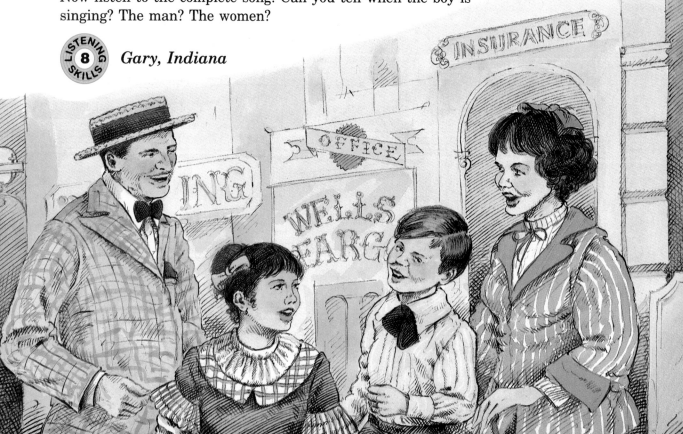

Growth Is Change

Your voice grows just as your body does. Although their unique qualities will stay about the same, most voices will become stronger as they grow older. Male voices will undergo an obvious change, and their ranges will often drop more than eight notes. As girls grow older, their more mature voices will have a richer, stronger quality.

Here are three young male voices singing excerpts from the same song. The first one has an unchanged voice like Winthrop's. The second voice is a changing voice and can often sing the higher tenor notes as well as the lower alto parts. The third voice is a young, changed-voice baritone. The final voice is a fully mature baritone singing the complete song.

H.M.S. Pinafore, "When I Was a Lad," three versions (excerpts, then complete version) ....Gilbert and Sullivan

After all, everyone is unique—so why should your voice sound the same, change at the same time, or change in the same way as anyone else's?

Tenor and Baritone

In this song there is a part for changing voices. It is written in the treble clef but sounds an octave (eight notes) lower. A part for baritone is also given. It is written in the bass clef where it sounds as written.

In the Evening by the Moonlight

Words and Music by James Bland

New Day, New Low Note (Sometimes)

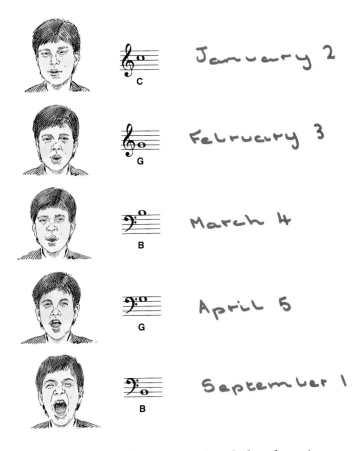

When male voices have completed the changing process, there still may be differences in quality and range among them. Often their parts are written differently as well—especially the tenor's.

As in the song on page 140, the tenor notes are written in the treble clef, but they sound eight notes lower in the bass clef.

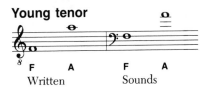

Baritone and bass parts are both written in the bass clef.

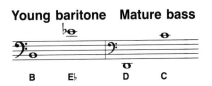

Girls' Voices

Female voices also change in range and quality, but in a less obvious way. The female voice will usually expand at both the bottom and the top of its range.

In these recordings, while both singers sing the same song, one is an adult woman and the other is a young girl. Both sing the song in the same range, but there are differences in quality. Can you describe these differences?

Coventry Carol . . . . .Traditional

Different types and styles of songs call for different kinds of voice production. Now that you have heard "Coventry Carol," try singing it yourself. Do you hear any differences between your voice and your classmates'?

Coventry Carol

Traditional English Carol   Words by Robert Croo

Boys and Girls Together

How would you sing "Shenandoah"? What clues do you get from looking at the music? What is there about the melody, dynamics, words, range, tempo, and the general mood of the music that can help you determine what kind of singing voice you should use?

Shenandoah

American River Shantey

1. Oh, Shen-an-doah, I long to hear you, — And — see _____ your roll-ing riv - er, ___ Oh, Shen-an-doah, I long to hear you, _____ A - way, _____ I'm bound a - way, 'Cross the wide Mis-sou - ri.

2. 'Tis sev'n long years since last I saw you,
   And heard your rolling river,
   'Tis sev'n long years since last I saw you,
   Away, I'm bound away, 'Cross the wide Missouri.

3. When first I took a rambling notion
   To leave your rolling river,
   To sail across the briny ocean,
   Away, I'm bound away, 'Cross the wide Missouri.

Singing in a Different Style

Since this is a different kind of song, you must change the style of
your voice. Will you sing with a lighter quality? A heavier quality?
Will you pronounce the words more precisely? More relaxed?

A Wonderful Day like Today

Words and Music by Leslie Bricusse and Anthony Newley

On a won-der-ful day __ like to-day __ I de-fy an-y cloud __
__ to ap-pear in the sky, __ Dare an-y rain-drop to plop in my eye __
__ On a won-der-ful day __ like to-day. __ On a won-der-ful morn-
- ing like this __ When the sun is as big __ as a yel-low bal-loon, __
E-ven the spar-rows are sing-ing in tune __ On a won-der-ful morn-ing like this. __
__ On a morn-ing like this __ I could kiss ev-'ry-bod-y, I'm
so full of love __ and good-will. __ Let me say fur-ther-more, __ I'd a-

dore ev-'ry-bod-y to come and dine, The pleas-ure's mine and I will pay the bill! May I

take this oc-ca - sion to say _____ That the whole hu-man race _____ should go

down on its knees, _____ show that we're thank - ful for morn-ings like these, _____ For the

world's in a won - der-ful way _____ On a won-der-ful day _____ like to - day. _____

Solo and Choral Singing

From your range chart, you know how high and how low you can
sing. Some of the notes you have on your chart might not be too
comfortable. The high pitches may sound thin, and the low pitches
raspy. Usually the best-sounding pitches will classify a voice as
soprano, alto, tenor, or baritone.

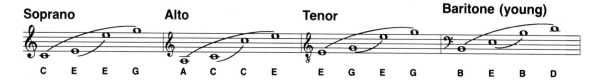

In this recording the same short familiar song is sung within the
ranges of each of the four voice classifications: soprano, alto, tenor,
and baritone. Sing along with each version of the song. The one that
feels most comfortable will determine your voice classification.

I've Been Working on the Railroad 🎱

Old American Work Song

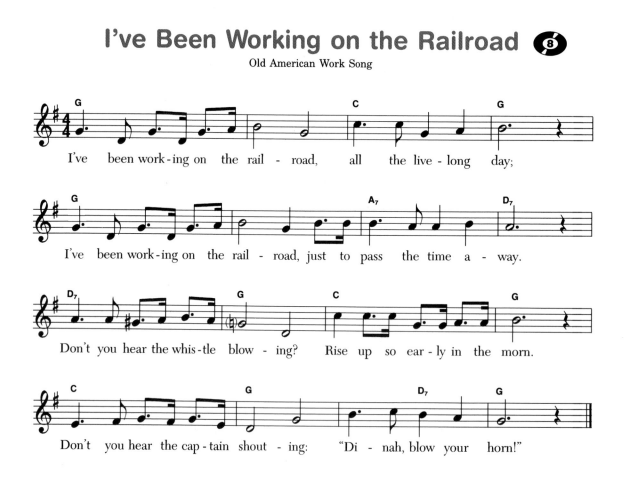

On Your Mark, Get Set, Breathe!

A vocal sound is made by directing air over the vocal cords or folds. The pitch of that sound is determined by the vibration of those cords as the air passes over them—the faster the vibration, the higher the pitch. You can breathe without making a noticeable pitch, but you can't sing or talk without breathing. Try this. Take a deep breath and hold it. When you took that breath, did you feel your waist and chest expand? Did you raise your shoulders?

Raising your shoulders doesn't help to get air into your lungs, but expanding your chest and your waist allows more space in the chest cavity for air. A tough muscle called a diaphragm looks like this when you are out of breath

OUT 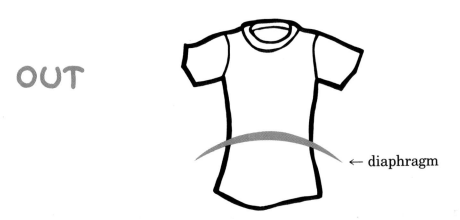 ← diaphragm

and looks like this when you expand to draw in a breath:

IN

In fact, it is the diaphragm that causes you to breathe in and out—even when you are asleep!

Developing Your Breath Control

You *think* you've taken a breath without raising your shoulders. To double-check, turn to your neighbor and have him or her place a hand on each of your shoulders. Now take a really deep breath and hold it. If your neighbor's hands do not rise, you are inhaling correctly.

Try this. Fill a paper cup with water and add a drinking straw. Take a deep breath without lifting your shoulders. Now blow gently through the straw and watch the bubbles surface in the cup. Try short spurts as well as a long, continuous exhaling. To sing long phrases, a singer must be able to exhale with a long, continuous stream of air. Test yourself. See how long you can keep the bubbles going on one breath of air. Try for longer and longer periods of exhaling.

Some kinds of singing use up the breath faster than other kinds. Singing loudly requires more breath flowing past the vocal cords. Whenever you have to sing lots of words very rapidly, you will use breath faster, since the act of pronouncing the words requires extra breath.

Compare the recording of "Rejoice Greatly, O Daughter of Zion," with "Lift Ev'ry Voice and Sing," both on page 150. In the first one the singer has to sing many notes in a very short time. In the second one the singers do not have to sing so many notes, but the slowness of the song requires good breath control. In both songs the composers have created long phrases of music between each breath.

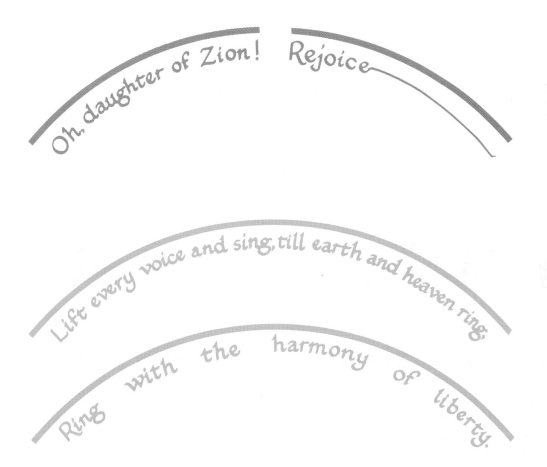

When you have heard both selections, try singing "Lift Ev'ry Voice and Sing." You will need to be conscious of the length of each phrase so you can reserve enough breath to sing to the end.

Messiah, "Rejoice Greatly, O Daughter of Zion" (excerpt) ....Handel

O daugh-ter of _ Zi - on! re - joice, _____ re - joice, _____

re - joice! _____

Lift Ev'ry Voice and Sing

Words by James Weldon Johnson   Music by J. Rosamond Johnson
Arranged by Albert McNeil

Maestoso

1. Lift ev - 'ry voice and sing, till earth and heav - en ring, ring with the
2. Ston - y the road we trod, bit - ter the chas - t'ning rod felt in the

har - mo - nies of lib - er - ty. Let our re - joic - ing
days when _ hope un - born _ had died. Yet with a stead - y

rise, high as the lis - t'ning _ skies, let it re - sound   loud as the
beat have not our wea - ry _ feet come to the place   for which our

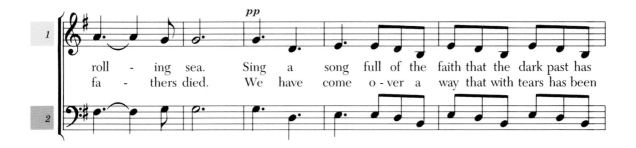

pp

roll - ing sea.   Sing   a   song full of the faith that the dark past has
fa - thers died.   We have   come o - ver a   way that with tears has been

molto cresc.   *allargando*   *f*

taught us;   Sing   a   song full of the hope that the pres - ent has brought   us;
wa - tered;   We have   come tread - ing our path thro' the blood of the slaugh - tered,

Tempo I
ff

Fac - ing the ris - ing   sun   of our new day be - gun, let us march
Out from the gloom - y   past,   till now we stand at ___ last where the white

on   till vic - to - ry _____   is   won.
gleam   of our bright star _____   is   cast.

151

Phrases

Composers often show where breaths can be taken by placing phrase lines above the notes. These are called slurs. Sometimes in the same song there are both short and long phrases. As you sing along with the recording, be sure not to take a breath until the end of each phrase line.

 8 *Spinning Wheel* . . . . David Clayton-Thomas

What goes up

must come down,

Spinnin' wheel

got to go 'round.

Talkin' 'bout your troubles, it's a cryin' sin,

Ride a painted pony, let the spinnin' wheel spin.

Ya got no money, and ya,

ya got no home,

Spinnin' wheel

all alone,

Talkin' 'bout your troubles and ya, ya never learn,

Ride a painted pony, let the spinnin' wheel turn.

Did you find a directing sign on the straight and narrow highway?

Would you mind a reflecting sign?

Just let it shine within your mind

and show you the colors that are real.

Someone is waitin'

just for you,

Spinnin' wheel

spinnin' true.

Drop all your troubles by the riverside,

Catch a painted pony on the spinnin' wheel ride.

The Warm-Up

Singing, like most physical activity, uses energy and needs physical preparation. Vocalizing with warm-up exercises gets the throat muscles and breathing apparatus ready for a performance.

Warming Up Your Own Voice

The best warm-up is done gradually. Start the warm-up softly, and get gradually louder. Also, begin it at a comfortable pitch and move gradually higher or lower. Then take a deep breath and hum a mid-range pitch softly. Hold the pitch for a comfortable length of time. Now, sing the melody below in the range that is comfortable for you. Try to sing the melody in one breath. Each time you sing it, go up one half-step, as shown in the sample. Use the syllable given or choose another that may be more comfortable for you.

Work up by half-steps with this second melody as well. It has a wider range. Can you sing this one in one breath?

Preparing for the Presentation

These additional warm-ups will help get you in shape for the big presentation.

Choral Warm-up

Some warm-ups help you tune up with other sections of the chorus. Here is a sample of this type of warm-up. Sopranos and altos sing this melody, using a syllable of their choice.

Warm-up No. 1

Now add baritones on this countermelody:

Warm-up No. 2

Try singing "Warm-up No. 1" and "Warm-up No. 2" together.

"Warm-up No. 3" can be sung by tenors and those altos who find "Warm-up No. 1" too high. It can be sung with Warm-ups No. 1 and 2.

Warm-up No. 3

Singing the three exercises together should aid your group's sensitivity to pitch as well as "warm you up" for singing.

The Presentation

Professional singers spend a great deal of time practicing their *presentation.* As you sing the song on page 155, decide how you can use your hands, body, and facial expression to help the audience understand what you are singing about.

Carolina in the Morning

Words by Gus Kahn   Music by Walter Donaldson

Noth - ing could be fin - er than to be in Car - o - li - na in the morn - ing,
Stroll - ing with my girl - ie where the dew is pearl - y ear - ly in the morn - ing,

No one could be sweet - er than my sweet - ie when I meet her in the morn - ing.
But - ter-flies all flut - ter up and kiss each lit - tle but - ter-cup at dawn - ing,

1. Where the morn - ing glo - ries twine a - round the door,
Whis-per-ing pret - ty sto - ries I long to hear _ once more.

2. If I had A - lad - din's lamp for on - ly a day, ___
I'd make a wish and here's what I'd say: — Noth-ing could be fin - er than to be in Car - o - li - na in the morn - ing.

Presentation-Plus

Presentation is not enough if no one can understand the words. Often, solos in a musical play are important to the understanding of the plot. Here, the "Music Man," Harold Hill, is trying to convince the town that unless they buy instruments for the youth and form a town band, the youngsters will get into bad habits. Even though you can't see the actor/singer, you have a very clear idea of the notion of the song. This is because he enunciates the words very clearly.

 "Ya Got Trouble" from *The Music Man* . . . . . . Willson

Sometimes it is not appropriate to use very much movement or exaggerated facial expression. Then, the singer must express the feeling of the music through clear enunciation of the words, correct voice quality, and proper use of dynamics (loudness and softness). Do you hear these things in "Caro mio ben"? Listen.

Caro mio ben

Words and Music by Giuseppe Giordani

With feeling

Ca - ro mio ben, cre - di - mi al - men, sen - za di te
kah - roh myoh behn kreh - dee-mee ahl-mehn sehn - tsah dee teh

lan - gui - sce il cor. Ca - ro mio ben, sen - za di te lan -
lahn - gwee-sheh eel kohr kah - roh myoh behn sehn - tsah dee teh lahn -

gui - sce il cor. Il tuo fe - del so - spi - ra o - gnor.
gwee - sheh eel kohr eel twoh feh-dehl soh - spee-rah oh-nyohr

Ces - sa, cru - del, tan - to ri - gor; Ces - sa, cru - del,
cheh - sah kroo - dehl tahn - toh ree - gohr cheh - sah kroo - dehl

tan - to ri - gor, tan - to ri - gor! Ca - ro mio ben, cre - di - mi al - men,
tahn - toh ree-gohr tahn - toh ree-gohr kah - roh myoh behn kreh - dee-mee ahl-mehn

Sen - za di te lan - gui - sce il cor. Ca - ro mio ben,
sehn - tsah dee teh lahn - gwee - sheh eel kohr kah - roh myoh behn

cre - di - mi al - men, sen - za di te lan - gui - sce il cor.
kreh - dee-mee ahl-mehn sehn-tsah dee teh lahn - gwee-sheh eel kohr

The Accompaniment

Listen to these two songs. You can easily hear the soloists singing the melody and the words, but what else do you hear?

 Ching-a-ring-Chaw..... ....Copland

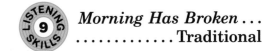 *Morning Has Broken...* ....Traditional

Many singers accompany themselves on guitar or piano. The chord symbols are placed above the melody in this song. You can perform "Morning Has Broken" or some other favorite piece as a solo, accompanying it with guitar, piano, or even autoharp. If you do not play these instruments, either a friend who does, or perhaps your teacher, can play an accompaniment for you. If neither one is available, a guitar and bass accompaniment is provided on the recording.

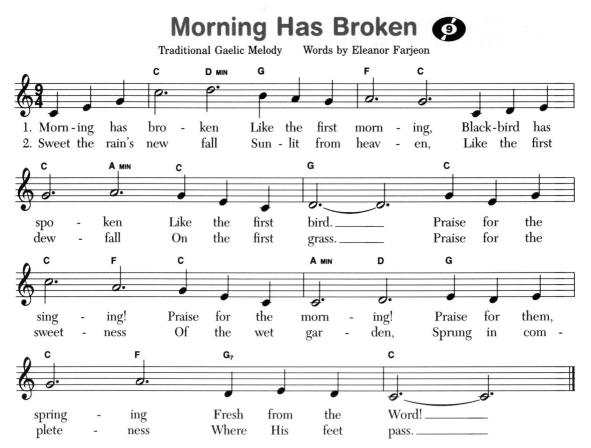

Copyright © 1957 by Eleanor Farjeon. Reprinted by permission of Harold Ober Associates Incorporated.

 "Morning Has Broken"—guitar and bass accompaniment

Singing in a Choral Ensemble

Finding Your Part

Although in some choral compositions everyone sings the same melody in *unison,* most ensemble singing is divided into voice parts. A full mixed chorus includes soprano, alto, tenor, and baritone or bass. A score for this combination usually looks like this:

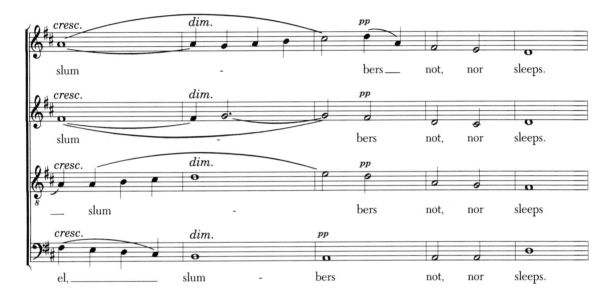

When each voice is printed on its own line, this is called *open score.* Often, if the voices do not move too independently, they are combined on one or two lines. This is called *closed score.* In the example below, the same piece you saw in open score has been redrafted to closed score. The sopranos and altos occupy the treble staff, and the tenors and baritones share the bass staff.

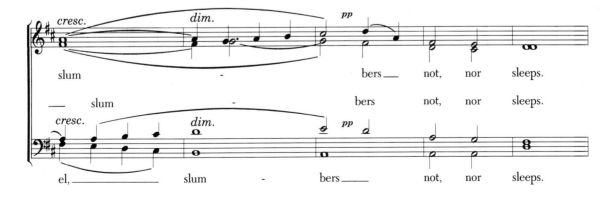

Setting Up a System

Often there are different voice groupings and ways of putting the parts on the staff. In this choral composition there are three voice parts: soprano, alto, and baritone. The soprano and alto parts share the treble clef. The baritone part has its own staff on the bass clef. When several staffs are written together it is called a *system,* and sometimes a *score*. Does the melody stay in the same part throughout the arrangement?

Look for the Silver Lining

Words by Bud de Sylva   Music by Jerome Kern   Arranged by Mary E. Hoffman

Following a Choral Score

In many choral scores each voice has its own staff. Sometimes all voices do not sing all the time. Here is an a cappella (unaccompanied) SATB composition. The arrows will help you follow the important entrances in the various voice parts.

Psallite

Music by Michael Praetorius   English Version by Dom Aylwyn Swithun, O.S.B.G.

Rhyming

In vocal music, words can create patterning that is not possible in instrumental music. One pattern device is rhyming.

In this song the *lyricist,* or the writer of the words, uses words that rhyme at the ends of lines; sometimes rhymes appear within the lines as well. Here are the lyrics only. Follow them as you listen to the recording.

Yesterday *John Lennon and Paul McCartney*

Yesterday, all my troubles seemed so far away,

Now it looks as though they're here to stay

Oh, I believe in yesterday.

Suddenly, I'm not half the man I used to be,

There's a shadow hanging over me,

Oh, yesterday came suddenly.

Why she had to go, I don't know,

She wouldn't say.

I said something wrong,

Now I long for yesterday.

Yesterday, love was such an easy game to play,

Now I need a place to hide away,

Oh, I believe in yesterday.

Patterns in Vocal Music

Patterns in music are created by different kinds of repetition.
Rounds repeat patterns by *imitation*. This round is written on four
staffs to show how the patterns in the first voice are imitated in the
other voices.

The Hall of Fame

Words Attributed to C. A. Alington   Music by Christopher Lefleming

Patterns of Words and Melody

Many folk songs share the pattern of words and melody. In "All My Trials," the verse words change but the refrain words stay the same. Usually, the verse melody is different from the refrain melody. In this song, the ending of the verse melody and the refrain melody are alike.

All My Trials

Spiritual from the West Indies

1. If re - li - gion was a thing that mon - ey could buy, _____
2. I _____ had _____ a _____ book, 'twas giv - en to me, _____
3. Oh, _____ Jor - dan _____ river is chill - y and cold. _____

— The rich would live _____ and the poor would die. _____
— And ev - 'ry leaf _____ spelled _____ vic - to - ry. _____
— It chills the body _____ but _____ not the soul. _____

All my tri - als, Lord, _____ soon be o - ver. _____

REFRAIN

Too late, my broth - ers. _____ Too late, but nev-er mind. _____

All my tri - als, Lord, _____ soon be o - ver. _____

168

"Refrain-First" Songs

In some folk songs the verse-and-refrain pattern is reversed to
create a slightly different form. In these kinds of songs, the refrain
is sung first and is followed by the verse. The refrain is then
repeated. If there are several verses, the refrain is repeated between
each verse and again at the end of the song. "Trampin'" is a good
example of this kind of "refrain-first" song. Can you find other
examples in your book?

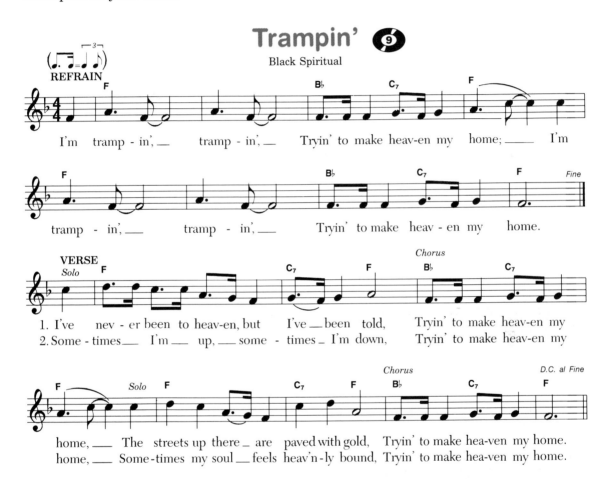

A Choral Score

Follow the choral score on page 170 as you listen to the composition.
How many different kinds of patterns can you find?

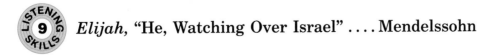

Elijah, "He, Watching Over Israel" .... Mendelssohn

He, Watching Over Israel

from *Elijah*

Felix Mendelssohn

LISTENING SKILLS 9

It Don't Mean a Thing if It Ain't Got That Swing........Ellington

They called it "swing"! And it did—from the early 1930s right up to the mid-1950s. Duke Ellington's popular 1932 recording of *It Don't Mean a Thing if It Ain't Got That Swing* gave the style its name, but all jazz musicians were a part of it, including, of course, Benny Goodman, who was called the King of Swing.

Vocal Music and the Dance Band

Almost all bands in the Swing era had vocal soloists. A few even had small choral groups, but none were of the caliber of the Fred Waring band. Waring introduced to the United States a brand-new sound in choral music—natural, popular, and youthful. It was Waring who first gave us the show choir. While Waring died in 1984, a group bearing his name is still touring today, continuing to spread his influence.

The Show Choir

Have you ever heard a show choir? In the past few years they have become popular in many schools. Perhaps you have a friend or a brother or sister who sings in a show choir. Perhaps you yourself are in a show choir!

Show choirs sing all kinds of popular music, including "oldies-but-goodies," rock tunes, jazz, ballads, and musical comedy. Every kind of popular song is fair game for today's show choirs. Some add movement and props such as scarves, balloons, batons, or canes to color their presentations. It can be a really exciting show! Show—that's an important word. *Show* is a big part of a show choir concert. The various segments of the concert are often grouped in sets of songs called *medleys*. The medley that begins on page 178 is made up of three songs from "the Roaring Twenties." Work out the routine, keeping in mind you're not just singing this arrangement—you're performing it! (If you happen not to be directly involved in one or more of the following routines, practice being an attentive, responsive member of the audience. Remember, appropriate expressions of support and appreciation are extremely important to the show and will bring out the best in the performers.)

Roaring Twenties

(Tip-Toe thru the Tulips with Me/Bye, Bye, Blackbird/Button Up Your Overcoat)

Arranged by Mary E. Hoffman

178

BYE, BYE, BLACKBIRD

Words by Mort Dixon   Music by Ray Henderson

BUTTON UP YOUR OVERCOAT

Words and Music by B. G. DeSylva, Lew Brown and Ray Henderson

You'll get a pain and ru - in your tum-tum! Keep a-way from col-lege kids _

You'll get a pain and ru - in your tum-tum! Keep a-way from col-lege kids _

when you're on a spree, Take good _ care of your-self, _ take good _

when you're on a spree, take good _

care of your-self, _ Take good care of your-self _ for me! _____

care of your-self, _ Take good care of your - self _ for me! _____

Let's Open with Pizzazz

Every good show needs an exciting opener—something that "knocks them out." "Another Op'nin', Another Show," on page 184, is a good one. You might think of others.

Another Op'nin', Another Show

from *Kiss Me Kate*

Words and Music by Cole Porter

The Novelty Number

Every show needs a change of pace. Following an upbeat chorus tune like "Another Op'nin', Another Show" with a soft, slow ballad sung by a soloist is a logical step. But here is a change of pace that can be made with a funny little twist. As the soloist sings, various people walk behind him or her wearing "ugly face" masks. At the end, one of the "ugly faces"—a girl, if the singer is a boy; a boy, if the singer is a girl—puts his or her "face" right next to the soloist, who unsurprised, smiles and kisses the "ugly face's" nose!

If the soloist is a boy, he should sing *her face*. If the soloist is a girl, she should sing *his face*.

I've Grown Accustomed to Her Face ⑨

from *My Fair Lady*

Words by Alan Jay Lerner   Music by Frederick Loewe

I've grown ac - cus-tomed to her face,_____ She al-most makes the day be-gin. _____

— { I've grown ac-cus-tomed to the tune she whis - tles night and noon; Her
   I've got - ten used to hear her say, "Good morn -ing" ev - 'ry day; Her

smiles, her frowns, her ups, her downs }
joys, her woes, her highs, her lows } are sec-ond na -ture to me now, _____

— Like breath-ing out and breath-ing in. _____ { I was se -
                                                  I'm ver - y

rene - ly in - de - pen-dent and con - tent be - fore we met; Sure - ly I could
grate-ful she's a wo - man and so eas - y to for - get; Rath - er like a

al - ways be that way a - gain, and yet, I've grown ac-cus-tomed to her looks, ac -
hab - it one can al-ways break, and yet, I've grown ac-cus-tomed to the trace of

rit.   **1.**   *a tempo*   **2.**

cus-tomed to her voice, }
some-thing in the air, } Ac-cus-tomed to her face. I've grown ac - face.

Let's Give the Music a Hand (Motion-wise, That Is)

A good way to make a show number even more effective is to add hand motions. You learned this song on page 134. This time your teacher will help you work out hand motions to go with "I Want to Be Happy."

I Want to Be Happy

from *No, No, Nanette*

Music by Vincent Youmans   Words by Irving Caesar   Arranged by Mary E. Hoffman

gray and you say you are blue, I'll send the sun smil - ing

gray and you say you are blue, I will send the

through. _____ I want to be hap - py, but I won't

sun - shine to you. I want to be hap - py, but I won't

be hap - py till I make you hap - py, too. _____

be hap - py till I make you hap - py, too. _____

Hand Motions

It helps to remember hand motions if you know exactly where the hand motions go in the music. Considering that your motions will be on the beat, let's see how the lyrics and the beats coincide. (The *x* represents the beat.)

```
x         x        x        x        x        x         x       x
I  want       to   be       happy,  But  I       won't  be      happy,

x         x        x        x        x        x         x       x
Till  I       make you      happy,  too! _____
```

There is a pattern of movements you can work out with this song. Your teacher, or someone who knows the pattern, will show it to you.

Knees and Toes, That's How It Goes

Adding motions with your knees and your feet will lend a lot of spark to any performance. With feet together and standing in place, try this 4-beat pattern.

First beat—Turn slightly left and bend your knees.

Second beat—Straighten up.

Third beat—Turn slightly right and bend your knees.

Fourth beat—Straighten up.

Simple, isn't it? Practice it a few times, and try it on one of the phrases of "I Want to Be Happy."

Toe-Tapper

Fancy footwork always adds an extra dash! This one is easy. Stand up and put your weight on your left foot. Keeping your right heel on the floor, tap your right toe to the right, then to the center. Do this on the beat several times. Now try it with the left foot—left, center, left, center, and so on.

Here's a toe-tap pattern you can use as a *vamp* (a "swing" way to say *introduction*). R = right; C = center; L = left.

R　C　R　C　　L　C　L　C

R　C　L　C　　Click heels on each beat

Sidewinders

Are you tired of doing all your steps while facing front? Try a sidewinder. Turn your body so you face stage left; your right side will be to the front of the stage. Now follow these simple steps:

1. Tap your right toe to *your* front (extend as far as you can).
2. Tap your toe out to *your* right (to stage front).
3. Tap your toe behind you (again, extend as far as you can).
4. Bring your feet together.
5. Reverse, with your left side to stage front.

191

The Offbeat Shuffle

"Let's face it. That's the most offbeat suggestion I've ever heard."
"I'm not comfortable with it. It's a little too offbeat for me."

When we use the term *offbeat,* we usually mean something unusual, something out of the ordinary. In music, *offbeat* has a "not-quite-so" meaning. It means that certain beats are stressed, or accented, that wouldn't be normally. Look at this pattern of quarter notes in $\frac{4}{4}$ meter. Normally they would be stressed like this:

But in an offbeat shuffle, one of the accents may be placed on a beat that wouldn't ordinarily carry it, like this:

Or this:
etc.

It isn't syncopation, exactly; it's more like putting the accent on the wrong syl-LA-ble. (And, of course, you can see the misplaced accent isn't *off* the beat at all. It's certainly on a beat, just not the expected one!)

When stepping an offbeat shuffle, you'll see it's easy. The feet step backward and forward, and all you have to do is remember which foot stamps loudly.

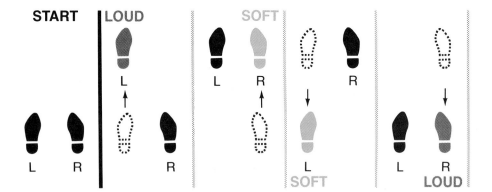

The Jazz Square

Here's another easy foot pattern. All you do is make a square with
your foot:

Start.

**First beat—Step right with the right foot and lean
slightly right.**

**Second beat—Step in front of the right foot with the
left foot, and lean slightly forward.**

**Third beat—Cross the right foot over the left foot and
lean slightly forward.**

**Fourth beat—Slide the left foot behind the right foot
and straighten your body.**

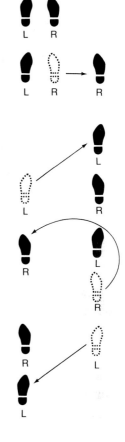

Repeat by simply sliding your right foot to the right, back to the
starting position.

Putting It All Together

In the 1930s a choreographer (kohr ee AH grah fur) named Busby Berkeley became famous in Hollywood movies for his lavish musical and dance productions, most of which cost millions of dollars to produce. You can work out a production number that won't cost you anything except some time and effort. First, learn to sing this song.

Singin' in the Rain

Words by Arthur Freed   Music by Nacio Herb Brown

I'm sing - in' in the rain, just sing - in' in the rain; What a glo - ri-ous feel - ing, I'm hap - py a - gain! I'm laugh - ing at clouds so dark up a - bove, The sun's ___ in my heart ___ and I'm read - y for love. Let the storm - y clouds chase ev - 'ry - one ___ from the place; Come on ___ with the rain, I've a smile ___ on my face! I'll walk down the lane with a hap - py re - frain, And sing - in', ___ just sing - in' in ___ the rain! _____

194

Move Over,
Busby Berkeley

Your teacher, or another student, will help you work out a movement sequence for "Singin' in the Rain." It will include a little of each movement pattern you've learned.

Propping Up the Show

Have you ever been in a play? If you have, you will know that anything you had to handle—a glass, a newspaper, a book, a flashlight—was called a *prop,* or *property.* In a swing choir, props can add lots of excitement and color.

Try making some hoops. Take a piece of heavy cardboard and cut out a circle 18 inches across.

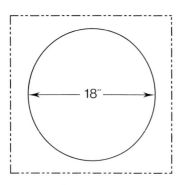

Now cut another circle 2 inches *inside* the original circle.

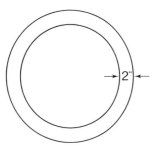

Knock out the center, and you have a hoop. Paint the hoops in different bright solid colors.

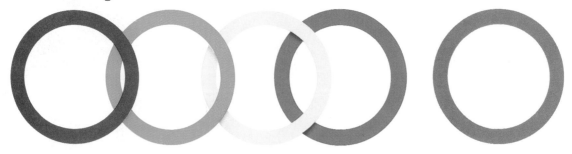

Your teacher, or perhaps another student, will show you some movements to do with your hoops.

We *Hoop* You Like Our Show

Work out your own hoop routine to "Me and My Shadow." The meter is $\frac{4}{4}$ and there are 32 measures, so you will need a routine that lasts 128 beats. If you break them down into eight 16-beat segments, it will be easier to work out. Remember, if you work out a routine to the recording, there will also be a 16-beat introduction.

Me and My Shadow

Words and Music by Bill Rose, Al Jolson, and Dave Dreyer

Me and my shad - ow, stroll - ing down the av - e - nue;_____ Me and my shad - ow, not a soul to tell our trou - bles to;_____ And when it's twelve o' - clock____ we climb the stair,____ we nev - er knock, __ __ for no - bod - y's there. ____ Just me and my shad - ow, all a - lone and feel - ing blue._____

Raising Cane

A cane is always good for adding tone color and movement. Holding the cane in your right hand, tap out this rhythm on the floor:

Make some taps louder than others:

Do the same thing with your left hand. Try tapping the pattern with the cane slanted away from you so that you tap on the edge of the tip rather than directly down on the tip.

Hold the top of the cane with both hands—the cane directly in front of you, the tip directly on the floor. Keep your feet slightly apart. Now sway left for 2 beats, then sway right for 2 beats.

sway sway sway sway
L   R   L   R

Now with your right hand on the tip of the cane and your left arm in the air in a waving motion, take eight small steps clockwise around the cane, returning on the eighth step to your original position. Change hands and do the same thing counterclockwise.

Learn to sing "Walkin' Along" on page 199. When you have it memorized, your teacher, or another student, will help you work out a cane pattern that will go with the song.

Walkin' Along

Words and Music by Mary E. Hoffman

Walk-in' a - long,_ just a-walk-in',_ sing-in' a song by _ my - self._ There is no - bod-y but me _ as I walk down the av - e - nue all a-lone, But I have a strange feel - in' that there's some-bod-y there,_ just a - walk-in'_ down the street, keeps me com-pan - y. You can't see {him her} walk-in' with me,_ right be-side me; who can it be? there be-side me,_ a - lone, Is it a phan - tom see? as I'm walk-in'_ a - lone. I glance, but there's no - bod - y there; I must be dream-ing. Walk-in' a - long,_ just a-walk-in',_ sing-in' a song by _ my - self._ But if you hap - pen to see _ an - y - bod - y walk - in' down the street with me, it's my shad - ow._

A Production Number

Busby Berkeley is back!

Make a production out of the hoop routine and the cane routine. First, put four girls on stage left and four boys on stage right, all in front of the chorus. The chorus sings "Me and My Shadow" as the girls do the hoop routine. The boys stand with their canes in front of them, both hands on top of their canes.

Adding a Partner

The interlude into "Walkin' Along" brings the girls to attention, their hoops held in both hands directly in front of them. The boys do the cane routine to "Walkin' Along."

Now the chorus sings "Me and My Shadow" and "Walkin' Along," as partner songs, and boys and girls repeat their routines at the same time.

On With the Show!

Well, here we are! In little more than two dozen pages, you have put together a show. Here's how the program looks:

ANYWHERE JUNIOR HIGH SCHOOL

presents

THE ANYWHERE SHOW CHOIR

directed by Les McMusick

1. *Another Op'nin', Another Show...*
   the big opener

2. *I've Grown Accustomed to Her Face...*
   solo novelty

3. *Roaring Twenties*...... 3 - in - 1 to triple
   your fun
   Button Up Your Overcoat
   Bye, Bye, Blackbird
   Tip-Toe Thru the Tulips

4. *I Want to Be Happy...* with a good hand
   for the singers

5. (One of your favorite songs)

6. *Me and My Shadow...* hoops and canes

7. *The Varsity Drag...* The Grand Finale

The finale is a well-known song from the Roaring Twenties—"The Varsity Drag." Work out a routine with sidewinders, offbeat shuffles, and jazz squares. As a grand finale, pick up canes on either side of the stage and go into the audience. Do the cane routine in the aisles to the last part of the song. Make sure your canes are high overhead at the end. As the audience applauds (long and loud, of course), shake hands with members of the audience. Then run down the aisles to the stage for one more bow.

YOU DESERVE IT, SO *BREAK A LEG!*

The Varsity Drag

Words and Music by B. G. de Sylva, Lew Brown, and Ray Henderson

1. Here is the drag, see how it goes; Down on the heels,
2. Hot-ter than hot, new-er than new! Mean-er than mean,
3. Down on the heels, up on the toes, Stay af-ter school,

last time to Coda

[1.]
up on the toes. That's the way to do the Var-si-ty Drag.____
blu-er than blue,
learn how it goes;

[2.]
Gets as much ap-plause as wav-ing the flag!_____ You can pass

man-y a class wheth-er you're dumb or wise, If you all

D.C. al
an-swer the call when your pro-fes-sor cries, "Ev-'ry-bod-y,

Coda
Ev-'ry-bod-y do the Var-si-ty, ev-'ry-bod-y

do the Var-si-ty, Ev-'ry-bod-y do the Var-si-ty Drag!"_____

Catching Crabs
by William Sidney Mount.

The Museums at Stony Brook, Stony Brook, New York.
Gift of Mr. & Mrs. Ward Melville.

Father and Son . . . . Cat Stevens

FATHER: It's not time to make a change,
just relax, take it easy.
You're still young, that's your fault,
there's so much you have to know.

Find a girl, settle down, if you want,
you can marry. Look at me, I am old
but I'm happy.

I was once like you are now, and
I know that it's not easy to be calm
when you've found something going on.
But take your time, think a lot, why,
think of ev'rything you've got;

204

For you will still be here tomorrow,
but your dreams may not.

SON: How can I try to explain? When
I do he turns away again.
It's always been the same, same old story.
From the moment I could talk I was
ordered to listen. Now there's a way,
and I know that I have to go away
I know I have to go.

FATHER: It's not time   SON: Away, away, away,
to make a change,   I know I have to
just sit down, take   make this decision
it slowly. You're   alone—no.
still young, that's
your fault, there's so much you have to go through. Find a girl, settle
down, if you want, you can marry. Look at me, I am old but I'm happy.

SON: All the times   FATHER: Stay, stay, stay,
that I've cried,   Why must you go and
keeping all the   make this decision alone?
things I knew inside.
It's hard, but it's
harder to ignore it. If they were right I'd agree,
but it's them they know, not me.
Now there's a way, and I know that I have to go away;
I know I have to go.

It Takes a Lot of Know-how to Set a Proper Text

When composers like Cat Stevens set
words to music, they must decide how
their melodies and harmonies will
capture the mood of the text. They
must select instruments that will sound
right for the song, they must choose a
proper tempo and dynamic level, and
they must pitch the song so that it can
be sung comfortably and effectively.
Some parts may lie in the high part of
the voice. Others may lie in the low part.

Schubert and the Erlking

Do you remember when we studied about the Romantic period we mentioned how much the Romantic composer was attracted to supernatural subjects? We heard *Danse macabre,* a description of a pretty spooky event!

In nineteenth-century Germany there were many, many legends about elves and witches and other ghostly creatures. (It was during this time that the Grimm brothers collected and wrote down the famous fairy tales.) *The Erlking*—a kind of concert song called a *lied* (LEEDT) in German—is Franz Schubert's response to the supernatural. Schubert believed the music and lyrics of a lied should be equally important. Each should support the other.

Death on a Pale Horse
by Albert Ryder.

The Cleveland Museum of Art, Purchased by Income J.H. Wade Fund.

The words to *The Erlking* are by a famous German poet named Goethe (GUHR tuh). As the legend goes, the Erlking, the king of the elves, could claim young children for himself if he could catch them. At his touch they would die. In the story, the Erlking chases a father and his young son riding on horseback through the night. Only the boy can hear the Erlking's taunts and jeers. The father thinks it is just the wind! The Erlking lures the boy with promises of gifts and games. Each time the boy cries out to his father, the child's voice rises in terror—until finally. . .

Follow the score of *The Erlking* on page 208 as you listen. While the singer sings the text in German, you can follow the English translation underneath the German words. As you listen, consider these questions:

1. There are four characters in this song—the father, the son, the Erlking, and the narrator. How does Schubert help the singer to show the differences between the four characters?

2. As the child calls out in fear, listen for this motive:

How does Schubert show the child's rising terror with this motive?

3. Schubert keeps a triplet rhythm () going nearly to the end to describe the hoofbeats of the horse. Does the rhythm ever change character? Where and how?

After all the heavy accompaniment, how does Schubert accompany the last two words, *war todt* ("was dead")?

Der Erlkönig (The Erlking) . . . . Schubert

207

Der Erlkönig

(The Erlking)

Music by Franz Schubert   Poem by Johann von Goethe
English Translation by Dr. Theodore Baker (Adapted)

Narrator *mf*

Wer rei - tet so spät durch
Who's rid - ing so late through

Nacht und Wind? Es ist der Va - ter mit
night and wind? It is a fa - ther who

sei - nem Kind; Er hat den Kna - ben wohl in dem
bears his child; And well the boy he folds in his

Arm___ er fasst ihn si - cher, er hält ihn
arm, ___ he clasps him close - ly, he holds him

warm.
warm.

mp Father

„Mein Sohn, was birgst du so bang dein Ge - sicht?"
"My son, why hide you your face now in fear?"

"Ich lie - be dich, mich reizt dei - ne schö - ne Ge -
"I love you so, how charm - ing you are, and so

stalt; Und bist du nicht wil - lig, so brauch' ich Ge -
fair; If you are not will - ing, my pow - er be -

walt." "Mein Va - ter, mein Va - ter, jetzt fasst er mich
ware!" "My fa - ther, my fa - ther! how i - cy his

an! Erl - kö - nig hat mir ein Leids ge -
clasp! Ah, how it hurts me, the Erl - king's

than!" Dem Va - ter grau - set's; er
grasp!" The fa - ther shud - ders, he

rei - tet ge - schwind, er hält in den Ar - men das
rides on a - pace, His child ev - er clasp - ing in

äch - zen - de Kind. Er - reicht den
clos - er em - brace; He reach - es

Hof mit Müh' und Noth: In sei - nen Ar - men das
home so filled with dread: With - in his arms, there the

Kind war todt!
child was dead!

211

Happy Birthday, Queen Mary!

When was the last time you had a birthday party? What did you eat? Did you play games? Did you sing? Many, many years ago, Queen Mary, who ruled England with her husband, William, celebrated a birthday. For that occasion in 1694, a young English composer, Henry Purcell, composed a piece of music called *Come, Ye Sons of Art*. There were several sections in the piece, and one section was a duet called "Sound the Trumpet." Here is the text.

Sound the trumpet till around
You make the list'ning shores rebound.

On the sprightly hautboy* play,   *oboe
All the instruments of joy that
skillful numbers can employ,
to celebrate the glories of this day.

What a curious text! What does it have to do with a birthday celebration? Look at the text closely. What words or phrases can you find that indicate this as a celebration piece?

As you follow the score of "Sound the Trumpet" on page 213, ask yourself, What did Purcell do to express his text? Did he do anything to capture the feeling of the trumpet? How does he make the word *sound* "sound" like sound?

Sound the Trumpet

from *Come, Ye Sons of Art*   Henry Purcell

Henry Purcell
(1659–1695)

Henry Purcell (PUHR s'l), like Mozart, lived only to his 36th year. From the beginning, this English composer showed an exciting talent. As a boy he sang in the chapel choir of King Charles II. When his voice began to change, he was made keyboard accompanist. You probably remember that Handel held a similar post at the Hamburg Opera. It was an enviable position for a very young musician to have, because it meant that the young person was being groomed for the position of conductor.

Purcell wrote in every musical form then popular in England. His music for the Church proved exactly right for the church-going English of the Baroque period. His works for small instrumental ensembles are still popular after 300 years. Purcell's theater pieces helped to build an audience for musical theater, which Handel would so successfully exploit later on.

Purcell's one true opera, *Dido and Aeneas,* is a very short work. Its three "acts" take less than an hour to perform. Purcell wrote it for a girls' school; and, indeed, only one part, that of Aeneas, is sung by a man. Although brief, the work is considered a masterpiece of English opera. Purcell's death marked the end of any significant English operatic composition until the twentieth century. The illustration is a scene from *Dido and Aeneas.*

Is It Singing?

Look at this dialogue. Read it as a play with another student.

GIRL: Come here! Come here right now!
BOY: What for? Why are you mad at me?
GIRL: You hid it. Don't say you didn't!
BOY: Hid what? What do you mean?
GIRL: I *saw* you. I *saw* you hide it.
BOY: Hide what? You couldn't see.
GIRL: (triumphantly) See what?
BOY: See what I. . . . Oh, no!

Now that you have spoken the dialogue, try speaking it in rhythm.
Listen for the chords in the piano. Say the words, using the rhythm
written in the score.

Spoken Recitative

Words and Music by Lawrence Eisman

Now try *singing* the words on pitch. You only have to use one or two pitches. Listen to the chords played on the piano and pick one or two to sing your words on.

This kind of speech-song is called *recitative* (reh see tah TEEV). On the recording you will hear how Gilbert and Sullivan combine spoken dialogue, recitative, and a call-and-response song all in one scene—in their operetta *H.M.S. Pinafore*. How does the recitative in the operetta differ from the spoken recitative you have performed?

H.M.S. Pinafore, "My Gallant Crew" . . . . Gilbert and Sullivan

A Theme Musical by Carmino Ravosa

Have you ever thought of putting on a talent show, a variety show? You can, you know.

The following songs can act as a beginning, a middle, and an end for your show. You can fill up the rest with comedy skits, songs, dances, TV commercials, pantomime to the accompaniment of rock records, instrumental solos—whatever—and you have a show. You may have budding rock stars, skit writers, and masters of ceremonies—right there in your own class. Here's the time to give them a chance to "shine."

Your show can be as big or as small as you want. It can be on stage before a large audience or in your classroom, with only your classmates as participants. You can have fancy costumes or just wear everyday clothing. You can have makeup, and scenery, or you can leave all that to your imagination. (Just change the words in the opening song, "Let's Put On a Show," to reflect your choice.)

Here is a bright show-biz opener for you. It can be sung by a soloist with the cast echoing the words and music. It can also be done by two soloists—one echoing the other.

Let's Put On a Show 🔟

Words and Music by Carmino Ravosa

© 1985 Carmino Ravosa

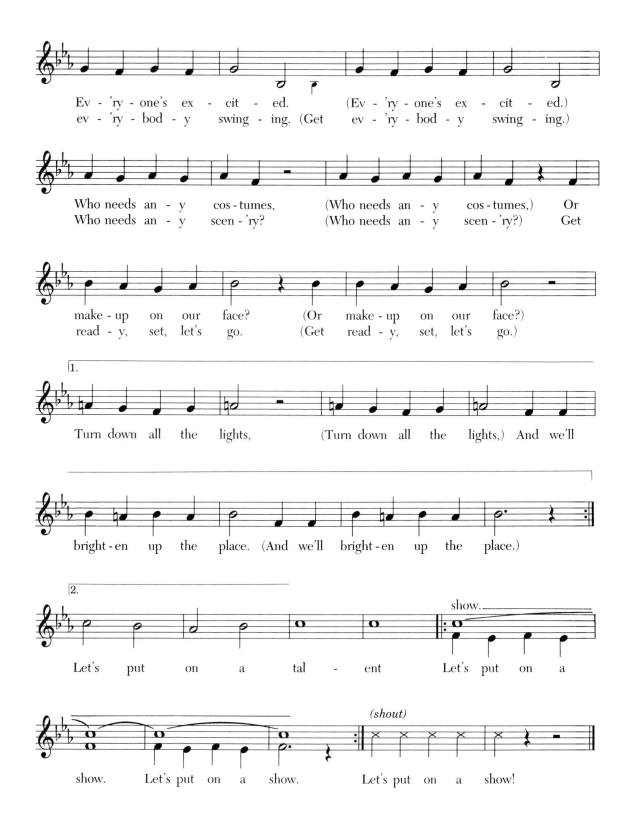

Ev - 'ry-one's ex - cit - ed. (Ev - 'ry-one's ex - cit - ed.)
ev - 'ry-bod - y swing - ing. (Get ev - 'ry-bod - y swing - ing.)

Who needs an - y cos - tumes, (Who needs an - y cos - tumes,) Or
Who needs an - y scen - 'ry? (Who needs an - y scen - 'ry?) Get

make - up on our face? (Or make - up on our face?)
read - y, set, let's go. (Get read - y, set, let's go.)

1.
Turn down all the lights, (Turn down all the lights,) And we'll

bright - en up the place. (And we'll bright - en up the place.)

2.
show.
Let's put on a tal - ent Let's put on a

show. Let's put on a show. (shout) Let's put on a show!

After the opening, have a master or mistress of ceremonies take
over to introduce songs and skits.

219

A Show-Biz Tradition

Now here's something for the middle of the show.

As a student is coming up to the stage to sing, have another student wish him or her "good luck." The rest of the company reacts in shock to the words "good luck." Then someone says "We don't say 'good luck.' In show biz we say 'break a leg.'"

Break a Leg

Words and Music by Carmino Ravosa

Freely
Solo

You won't ev - er lay an egg. Don't say "good luck," say

a tempo
Chorus

"break a leg." So, "break a leg!" That's a show biz good luck __ to

1.
you. __

2.
"Break a leg!" That's a

Solo

Chorus

show biz good luck __ to "Break a leg!" That's a

(Shout)

show biz good luck __ TO YOU!

221

The Old Soft Shoe

A soft-shoe makes a typical variety show act. After a few skits and a
rock song, a student could say "Hey, that's not my idea of music.
Give me the old times and the old tunes."

No Times like the Old Times

Words and Music by Carmino Ravosa

"Ricky-tick"

1. There're no tunes like the old tunes, No moons like the old moons,
no folks like the old folks, No jokes like the old jokes,

No times like the old times for me._____ 2. There're me._____
No times like the old times for

— Do you re-mem-ber those ev-'nings with those ster-e-op-ti-con

slides? And when I think of a trol-ley, brings a tear to my eyes. There're

no steps like the old steps, I'm sure you'll a-gree, There're

2nd time to ⊕ Coda

no times like the old times for me.

D.S. al ⊕

Do you re-

⊕ *Coda*

me.

222

It seems as if everyone loves a song-and-dance man. Do you want some more oldies? Here are some.

"Button up Your Overcoat"
"Bye, Bye, Blackbird"
"I Know That You Know"
"I Want to Be Happy"
"The Sidewalks of New York"
"Tip-Toe thru the Tulips"

By now you should be getting to the end of your show. Has everyone had a chance to act, sing, dance or write?

For the finish, pick a big song for the "eleven o'clock spot" (that's just before the ending). Then go on to the closing number, which is "Let's Put On a Show" with a change of lyric. You should sing the underlined words on the beat.

"Hope You Liked Our Show"

Hope you liked our show, (hope you liked our show)
It was great to do it;
Hope you liked our show;
We're happy we went through it.

It wasn't always easy,
But it was always fun;
It was lots of work;
Now we're sorry that it's done.

Hope you liked our show;
We loved every minute;
Hope you liked our show;
We loved being in it.

There were many times when
We thought that we would quit;
Now just look, we've got a hit.

Take your bows here. If there are individual bows, keep them moving rapidly. Your accompanist should keep playing the music of "Hope You Liked Our Show" while the curtain calls are being taken. Then, for an encore, begin singing the last seven lines, beginning with *Hope you liked our show/We loved every minute,* but at the line where you would sing *There were many times when,* sing instead:

We hope you've had a few laughs;
We hope we've made you smile;
Then our show was all worthwhile.

Chapter 8—Carmen, by Georges Bizet

Going to the Opera

Carmen
opera in four acts
by
Georges Bizet

libretto by
Meilhac & Halévy
from the novel by
Prosper Mérimée

⚍ Characters ⚍

MORALES (moh RAH lehs)
.... *an officer in the Guard*

MICAELA (mee kah AY lah)
.... *a girl from Don Jose's village*

DON JOSE (do[n] zhoh ZEH)
.... *a corporal of the Guard*

ZUNIGA (soo NEE gah)
.... *the Captain of the Guard*

CARMEN (KAHR mehn, *or* kahr MAYN)
.... *a gypsy girl*

FRASQUITA (frahs KEE tah)
MERCEDES (mehr SAY dehs)
.... *Carmen's friends*

LILLAS PASTIA (LEE lahs PAHS tyah)
.... *an innkeeper*

ESCAMILLO (ehs kah MEEL yoh)
.... *the toreador*

EL DANCAIRO (el dahn kah EE roh)
EL REMENDADO (el reh mehn DAH doh)
.... *smugglers*

soldiers, factory girls, street boys, gypsies,
smugglers, townspeople

WHY OPERA? The drama is so strong emotionally that only music can fully express it.

WHAT IS OPERA?

A play that is sung.

WHY ARE THE VOICES SO DIFFERENT FROM POPULAR ARTISTS' VOICES? They must be large voices that can be heard at great distance, because most opera houses use no amplification.

"TAKE THE HOUSE TO HALF"

That's the instruction by the stage manager to the lighting engineer to dim the house lights by half. At that moment the opera is about to begin! You are settled in a plush seat, your program or libretto of *Carmen* in hand. As the lights go out, a hush falls over the audience. The conductor enters to a round of applause, bows, raises the baton, and . . .

> *PRELUDE*—The orchestra paints a vivid picture of the excitement of the bullring and the romantic toreador; it warns of the tragedy about to unfold. Turn the page and follow the line score for the Prelude to *Carmen*.

Act I

THE SCENE: A street in Seville: to one side, a factory; to the other, a guardhouse; time—1820.

You be the actors! Take the dramatic parts and listen to the singers when the music begins.

THE PLOT: Soldiers hang around the guardhouse; people mill about the street. Micaela approaches Morales and asks for Don José. The soldiers flirt with her, inviting her to wait with them. She becomes frightened and leaves.

A trumpet is heard in the distance. The relief guards, captained by Zuniga, march in, followed by a crowd of boys who mimic their military bearing. Among the relief guards is Don José.

Chorus of Street Boys

English Words by C. E. Culp   Music by Georges Bizet

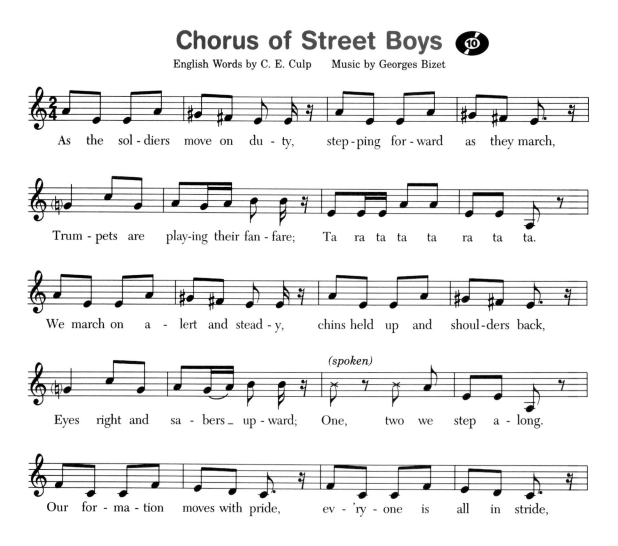

As the sol-diers move on du-ty, step-ping for-ward as they march,

Trum-pets are play-ing their fan-fare; Ta ra ta ta ta ra ta ta.

We march on a-lert and stead-y, chins held up and shoul-ders back,

(spoken)

Eyes right and sa-bers up-ward; One, two we step a-long.

Our for-ma-tion moves with pride, ev-'ry-one is all in stride,

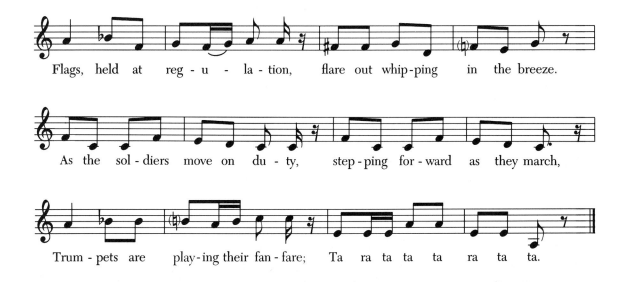

Flags, held at reg-u-la-tion, flare out whip-ping in the breeze.

As the sol-diers move on du-ty, step-ping for-ward as they march,

Trum-pets are play-ing their fan-fare; Ta ra ta ta ra ta ta.

AND <u>YOU</u> ARE ON STAGE!

(Don José and Zuniga move downstage)

ZUNIGA: Beautiful girls work in that factory!

DON JOSÉ: *(nonchalantly)* I haven't noticed.

A SOLDIER: I know why! It must be that charmer who was here looking for you.

DON JOSÉ: Micaela! *(Factory bell rings.)* Hear that? <u>You</u> look over the girls.

(Girls stream from factory, flirting. Don José is engrossed in making links for a chain.)

1ST SOLDIER: *(Looking toward factory)* I don't see her!
2ND SOLDIER: Where is Carmen?
OTHER SOLDIERS: Is she inside? Where is our gypsy?

(Carmen appears at the factory door, smiles flirtatiously at the men, and removes a red flower from her waistband.)

1ST SOLDIER: Look! There she is!
2ND SOLDIER: Carmen! Dance for us!
OTHER SOLDIERS: When will you say you love me? Come on, sing for us!
CARMEN: *(moving among the men, teasing with the flower, glancing often at Don José)* You want me to sing, dance, and tell you I love you? *(laughing)* I don't know when I'll be in love . . . maybe never!

Habanera

English Words by C. E. Culp   Music by Georges Bizet

As a bird in the for-est sings in free-dom, love-ly on the

wing, So is love as all na-ture flows, and it can

nev-er be tamed at all. Wait un-yield-ing; you hope in vain; No one is

bound, dreams are lost in pain. It's the qui-et one I pre-fer, tho' he's been

si-lent, I like him more. It's love! That's love!

Yes, love! Ah, love! Now, love is like a gyp-sy bold who must be

free, his rea-son to un-fold. I may love you if you don't

yield to me, Ah, love, I al-ways must be free. And if I

love you, be-ware for you be-long to me. So, if I

slowly

claim you for my own, then you'll be-long to me!

(Men gather around Carmen. She turns to Don José.)
CARMEN: *(coquettish)* What are you doing?
DON JOSÉ: Making a chain.
CARMEN: *(Flinging flower toward him, laughing)* Here's a chain that will hold you! *(Factory bell rings. Carmen and girls rush back to work. Others exit. Don José looks at the flower, picks it up, places it inside his jacket as Micaela appears.)*

• FOR STUDY •

In the original opera, Don José sings this recitative. You will hear it in French. Follow the English translation.

Don José's recitative (excerpt)

Quels re-gards! quelle ef-fron-ter - i - e!
What a sight! What a wick-ed wo - man!
Cet-te fleur
This ti - ny

là, m'a fait l'ef-fet d'u-ne bal - le qui m'ar-ri-vait!
flow'r made me to feel that I'd just ar-rived at a dance!

Andante moderato

Le par-fum en est fort et la fleur est jo - li - e!
Its per-fume fills the air and the blos-som is love - ly!

Et la fem - me? S'il est vrai - ment des sor -
And the wo - man? If it is true there are

ciè - res, C'en est u - ne cer-tai - ne - ment.
witch - es, there's no doubt that she must be one.

MICAELA: Don José! I stopped before—you weren't here. Your mother sent me with this letter, and a message.

DON JOSÉ: A message?

MICAELA: Yes. She asked me to tell you that she loves you and misses you. She sends you her blessing.

· FOR STUDY ·

In the original opera, Micaela sings a short aria describing the feelings of Don José's mother for her absent son. You will hear it in French. Follow the English translation.

Micaela's aria (excerpt)

Micaela

Et _____ tu lui di - ras que sa mè - re Son - ge
Tell _____ him that at noon and at night - time There's a

nuit et jour _____ a l'ab - sent, _____ Qu'el - le re - gret - te quèlle es -
moth - er lone - ly and sad, _____ That she re - grets, and that she's

pè - re, Qu'el - le par - don - ne et qu'el - le at - tend. _____ Tout ce - la n'est-ce par mi -
hop - ing, will - ing to wait and to for - give. _____ Have I not told you as she

gnon - ne, De ma part, tu le lui di - ras; _____ Et _____ ce bai - ser que je te
begged me, Told you all that she'd have me say; _____ Give _____ him this kiss as now I

don - ne, De ma part tu le lui ren - dras.
give you, It's a kiss that his moth - er gives.

(Don José is moved.)

DON JOSÉ: Will you wait while I read her letter?

MICAELA: No, you should read it alone.

DON JOSÉ: Will you come back?

MICAELA: I promise.

DON JOSÉ: *(looking at letter)* This is why she left. Very well. I will do as you wish, Mother, and marry Micaela. *(He folds the letter, places it inside his jacket; he touches the flower. His expression is troubled.)* As for that gypsy and her flower. . . .

(Don José is interrupted by screams from the factory. Zuniga and his soldiers rush toward the factory. Girls run out, calling for help. They say Carmen has had a fight with Manuelita. Some say Carmen started it; others blame Manuelita.)

(As the narrator speaks his lines, the performers mime the actions.)

NARRATOR: Zuniga sends Don José and a few soldiers to stop the disturbance. They return with a defiant Carmen, who refuses to answer Zuniga's questions. Zuniga remains polite, fascinated by her beauty. He assigns Don José to bind Carmen's hands and take her to prison.

Alone with Don José, Carmen boldly plots her escape. She is sure he will obey her wishes; her flower has already cast its spell.

Carmen entices him, softly singing the *Seguidilla,* telling of the inn where they might rendezvous. Although Don José struggles against her charm, his resistance weakens. He is captivated!

· F O R   S T U D Y ·

Here is how the scene goes in the original opera. Follow the music to hear how Bizet caught the action described by the narrator. The language is French, but you can follow the English translation.

10 *Au secours!* (excerpt)

C'est la Car-men-ci - ta!____ C'est el - le!
It's la Car-men-ci - ta!____

Non, non,__ ce n'est pas el - le! pas du
No! No!__ It was not Car - men! It was

si fait, si fait, c'est el - le! Elle a por - té____ les pré - miers
It was! It was that wo - man! She was the one____ to start the

tout!
not!

coups!__ Ne les é - cou - tez pas! Mon -
fight!__ Don't lis - ten to their talk! Mon -

(to Zuniga.)

Ne les é - cou - tez pas! E - cou - tez - nous, mon -
Don't lis - ten to their talk! Lis - ten to us, mon -

ff (to Zuniga.)

sieur! é - cou - tez - nous! é - cou - tez - nous! é - cou - tez - nous! é - cou - tez -
sieur, Lis - ten to us! Lis - ten to us! Lis - ten to us! Lis - ten to

sieur! é - cou - tez - nous! é - cou - tez - nous! é - cou - tez - nous!
sieur! Lis - ten to us! Lis - ten to us! Lis - ten to us!

nous! é - cou - tez - nous! é - cou - tez - nous, mon -
us! Lis - ten to us! Lis - ten to us, mon -

é - cou - tez - nous! é - cou - tez - nous, mon - sieur,
Lis - ten to us! Lis - ten to us, mon - sieur,

sieur, mon - sieur, é - cou - tez - nous!
sieur, mon - sieur, lis - ten to us!

mon - sieur, é - cou - tez - nous!
mon - sieur, lis - ten to us!

As the Narrator points out, Carmen entices Don José by singing the *Seguidilla* (a dance of southern Spain in triple meter). Listen to part of the *Seguidilla*. Can you hear the triple meter and the dancelike feel? The words are in French. Follow the English translation to hear what Carmen is singing to Don José.

Seguidilla (excerpt)

on s'en-nui – e, Et les vrais plai-sirs sont à deux;
be – ing lone – ly, Pleas – ures are best when shared by two;

Donc, pour me te-nir com-pa-gni-e, Je m'en-ne-rai mon a-mou-
And so to keep me com-pa-ny,___ I'll keep my sweet-heart by my

meno p (laughing.)

reux!___ Mon a – mou – reux
side!___ But now, you see,

il est au dia – ble, Je l'ai mis à la por - te
I have no sweet - heart, for yes - ter - day I threw him

hier! Mon___ pau – vre coeur très con – so –
out! My___ bro – ken heart needs con – so –

la – ble, Mon___ coeur est li – bre com – me l'air!
la – tion, My___ heart is free, as free___ as air!

NARRATOR: Don José, smitten by Carmen's charm, loosens the knot as Carmen explains her plan of escape. When the soldiers return, Don José will pretend to escort Carmen to jail. On the bridge, she will push him. He will fall as she escapes. Later they will meet at Lillas Pastia's inn.

As Act I concludes, the escape is completed. Carmen runs off, laughing, triumphantly flinging the rope in the air for all to see. Zuniga arrests Don José on the spot and the unfortunate corporal is taken to prison.

Act II

THE SCENE: Lillas Pastia's inn on the outskirts of Seville; the inn is a meeting place for smugglers. Carmen is a member of such a group.

THE PLOT: A month has passed. Gypsy women mingle with the soldiers. Carmen sits at a table downstage with Zuniga. She, along with her friends Frasquita and Mercedes, sings the "Gypsy Song." It concludes in a rousing gypsy dance.

Gypsy Song

English Words by C. E. Culp

Music by Georges Bizet

1. The music now begins to sound, ___ guitars and tambourines are
ver and copper rings now flash, ___ against the tawny skins they

sing - ing, with castanets the rhythm ring - ing,
gleam, ___ the skirts of orange red are shin - ing,

the ___ Gyp - sy ___ girls now start the dance. ___
a - float in the wind, they all de - light. ___

The puls - ing of the sound grows strong, as danc - ing feet move on the ground,
The dance, the song, be - come as one, the mu - sic sound - ing mad - ly now,

the tem - po throb - bing, pound - ing mad - ly, their voice in ___ song, ___
the step is slow, then fast - er mov - ing, with - out a ___ care, ___

rit.   *a tempo*

the ___ bod - ies ___ move, they whirl a - bout the room in bright ar - ray. ___
as ___ if in ___ air, then wild - er, bold - er, fast - er grows their dance! ___

Tra la la la, _____ tra la la la, _____

tra la la la, _____ tra la la la la la la la. _____

Frasquita, Mercedes, Carmen

Tra la la la, _____ tra la la la, _____

tra la la la, _____ tra la la la la la la

1.
2
2.

la. _____ Sil - la. _____

EL DANCAIRO: *(to Lillas Pastia)* Lillas, we have to have a meeting about the next smuggling job. Close the inn.

LILLAS PASTIA: Yes. At once. *(to the patrons)* All right, everyone. It's closing time. *(The patrons, grumbling, begin to gather their things to leave.)*

ZUNIGA: *(to Carmen)* You know, Don José has been released from prison.

CARMEN: *(smiling to herself, aside)* Has he? *(to crowd)* Good night, everyone.

(As the patrons say their good-nights, a commotion is heard outside. People are crying "Viva el torero" and "Long live Escamillo!")

ZUNIGA: They are cheering the toreador Escamillo. I think they're coming to the inn.

(El Dancairo and El Remendado glance at one another nervously. They are anxious to have their meeting.)

A PATRON: Escamillo is coming here!

(Enter Escamillo and his entourage to the introduction of the "Toreador Song.")

Toreador Song

English Words by C. E. Culp   Music by Georges Bizet

Here's a toast to ev - 'ry one of you, _____ Se -

ñors, se - ñors! ____ for all your brav - er - y.

Here's to the bull - ring, __ here's to the mat - a - dor, __

You de - light us in the ring, your style and __ your charm.

Sing "O - lé!" _____ the ring __ now is full, _____ the

ring is packed _____ from floor to roof. Ev - 'ry - one watch - ing __

is so ex - cit - ed. ___ How they shout and yell at one an -

oth - er, now it's a roar! More are greet - ing, and

oth - ers scream - ing __ As they raise __ their voi - ces to the top!

They a-wait __ a show to them ap-peal - ing, 'Tis the day __ they've wait-ed for! *O-lè!* On guard! *O-lè!* Let's go! Ah! __

To - re - a-dor, on guard, to-re - a-dor! To - re - a-dor! To - re - a-dor! Now think of flash-ing eyes all watch-ing you, Those dark eyes watch-ing you. __ As one will yield to you, To - re - a - dor, love waits, love waits for you!

ESCAMILLO: *(to Carmen)* What is your name, beautiful señorita?

CARMEN: My name is Carmen. Sometimes they call me Carmencita.

ESCAMILLO: I think I love you, Carmen.

CARMEN: *(casual but coy)* I doubt I love you.

ESCAMILLO: *(confidently)* You will! You'll be at my bullfight, Carmencita!

LILLAS PASTIA: Now everyone must go!

(Escamillo exits with the crowd.)

ZUNIGA: *(loitering after others have departed)* I'll return for you later, Carmen.

CARMEN: That would be a mistake!

ZUNIGA: *(exiting)* I'll take that chance!

EL DANCAIRO: *(to assembling smugglers)* I have a perfect scheme for our next job.

CARMEN: Count me out. I'm waiting here for someone.

EL DANCAIRO: We need you! For what reason do you stay here?

CARMEN: Love is my reason! A soldier was sent to prison because of me, and I expect him tonight.

(Don José's voice is heard in the distance, singing.)

LISTENING SKILLS 11 *Halte-là!*

Don José. *(offstage)*
(the voice approaches little by little.)

Hal - te - là! Qui va là! Dra - gon d'Al - ca - la! _____
Have a care! Who goes there? Man of Al - ca - la! _____

Où t'en vas - tu par là, Dra - gon _____ d'Al - ca - la? _____
Where are you go - ing there? Man of _____ Al - ca - la?

Ex - act et fi - dè - le, _____ Je vais ou m'ap - pel - le
Ev - er true and ten - der, _____ Faith - ful - ly I wan - der

L'a - mour de ma bel - le! S'il en est ain - si,
To my sweet-heart yon - der! If that is your aim,

Pas - sez, mon a - mi. _____ Af - fai - re d'hon - neur, _ Af - fai - re de
Pass the line my friend! _ When 'tis hon - or calls, _ Or _____ love _____ that en-

(Enter Don José.)

coeur, Pour nous tout est là, _____ Dra - gons d'Al - ca - la!
thralls, Com - rades all we are, _____ Men of Al - ca - la!

EL DANCAIRO: We can always use another!

CARMEN: He's a soldier; he would never join us! *(hesitating)* Still, I'll see what I can do. *(Smugglers exit. Don José enters, still singing. He stops when he sees her. Carmen moves to him, smiling.)* José!

DON JOSÉ: *(taking her hands in his)* Carmen . . . I have waited so long . . . I love you!

CARMEN: *(teasing)* Before you arrived, I was dancing for Zuniga and some officers.

DON JOSÉ: *(angry)* Zuniga? Here? With you?
CARMEN: You're jealous! Listen, José. I want to dance for <u>you</u>.
(Taking her castanets, she begins.)

· FOR STUDY ·

The following lines enclosed in the border may be used for performance as well as study.

As you listen to these words from the original opera that follow the dance, be aware that the English translation given here has the same rhythm as the French words sung on the recording. This should make it easier for you to follow.

 Carmen's dance, and *Duet*

DON JOSÉ: Listen a bit, Carmen, just for a bit! Please stop now!
CARMEN: What is wrong, if you please?
DON JOSÉ: Can you hear it? Down there. Yes, they're calling retreat. The bugles sound so clearly. You surely hear them, too.
CARMEN: Bravo! Bravo! This is his thank-you! I try, but he is bored with all my singing and dancing. And now he hears the trumpet, like a gift from the sky! *(continuing to dance)*
DON JOSÉ: Did I not make it clear, Carmen, I hear the bugle! It sounds for me—it calls me before lights are out.
CARMEN: To your camp? For retreat? Ah! I'm really such a blockhead!

CARMEN: Run, soldier, you wouldn't want to be late. And to think that I almost fell in love with you.
DON JOSÉ: *(pleading)* I don't <u>want</u> to leave.
CARMEN: *(taunts)* Ta-ra-ta-ta! The bugle sounds; he must rush off! This is the way he shows his love!
DON JOSÉ: You don't believe I love you?
CARMEN: Of course not! Run . . . you'll be late!
DON JOSÉ: Listen to me!
CARMEN: *(defiantly)* I won't!
DON JOSÉ: *(holding her arm)* <u>Yes, you will!</u> *(taking out the withered flower)* Let me explain.

243

As you listen to Don José sing his aria, "The Flower Song," follow the words in the score. The words are in French, but you can follow the English words to hear what Don José is saying to Carmen.

11 *Flower Song*

If you are performing the script, you can use this music as background music for Don José's words to Carmen. Keep the music low, so that Don José will be clearly heard by the audience.

DON JOSÉ: When I was in prison, I kept this flower with me, the flower that you threw to me. After a while, the petals dried and they lost their color. But even the fragrance reminded me of you. *(Carmen seems touched by his sincerity, but relentlessly continues.)*
CARMEN: *(softly)* If you really loved me, you wouldn't go back to camp. You would come with me. You would live like a gypsy. We would be free together! You wouldn't take orders from officers. We make our own laws.
DON JOSÉ: *(protesting)* Stop this! I cannot become a deserter!
CARMEN: *(angry)* Then go! <u>Now</u>. *(moving toward door)*
DON JOSÉ: *(moving to Carmen)* Listen to me. We <u>will</u> find a way.
CARMEN: *(moving away from him, furious)* I said <u>go</u>! I hate you! *(eyes fixed upon him)* <u>Goodbye</u>—forever!
DON JOSÉ: *(slowly walking to door)* As you wish. *(turning to Carmen, quietly)* Goodbye. *(A knock is heard.)*
CARMEN: *(hushed)* Stand back!
ZUNIGA: *(from outside)* Carmen! *(pushes open the door; sees Don José with Carmen.)* You're wasting your time with a <u>common</u> <u>soldier</u>! *(Moves to José.)* You, soldier, get out!
DON JOSÉ: *(determined)* I'm staying!
ZUNIGA: *(Strikes José.)* Who do you think you are? Get out!
DON JOSÉ: *(quickly drawing his sword)* I'll kill you! *(Zuniga draws his sword.)*
CARMEN: *(Calls smugglers.)* Help! Hurry! *(Smugglers rush in, seize Zuniga.)*
EL DANCAIRO: *(with mocked politeness)* If you please, sir! *(taking his sword)*
CARMEN: *(to Zuniga)* I warned you not to return.
EL DANCAIRO: *(with a pistol pointed at Zuniga's head)* We leave now. *(motioning toward door)* You must join us!
ZUNIGA: I'm leaving—and I will not forget this! *(looking at both Don José and the smugglers)*
EL REMENDADO: You walk ahead. *(bowing and pointing guns at Zuniga)*
CARMEN: You will be free soon! *(Zuniga and smugglers leave; Carmen turns to Don José.)* And now, will you come with me?
DON JOSÉ: *(resigned, sitting)* I have no choice.
CARMEN: You aren't overjoyed! But, once you know our world of freedom, you will love our life!
(Don José remains silent. All others join Carmen in rousing finale.)
ALL: We must be free! The land is ours! Our own law! Freedom!

The recording of the *Prelude* can be played as a curtain cue.

Act III

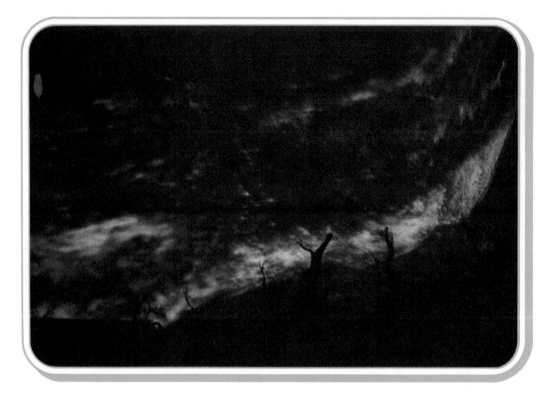

THE SCENE: The smugglers' mountainside hideaway near Don José's home.

 *Entr' acte*

(El Dancairo directs the smugglers as they quietly prepare to move goods. Some are seated, tying bundles; others stealthily begin to move down a narrow path. A few rest; all remain alert, cautious lest their location be discovered. Frasquita and Mercedes sit quietly playing cards by a fire. Don José stands apart from the others, gazing into the valley below. Eventually, Carmen approaches him.)

Music fades here.

CARMEN: Why do you stand here away from us? What are you watching?

DON JOSÉ: *(sadly)* My mother lives in this valley. She still believes her son is an honest, proud soldier. I am sick with guilt.

CARMEN: *(haughtily)* Why don't you go home, then? Go to your mother. This life with our band isn't working for you. The sooner you leave, the better for everyone!

DON JOSÉ: *(fired with jealousy)* That would suit your plans, wouldn't it? Is there someone else? *(she tosses her head)* If you tell me to leave one more time, I'll . . .

CARMEN: *(interrupting José)* What? You'll kill me? *(he stares at her)* Don't answer! My fate is written in the cards—nothing will change that. *(Turns from him abruptly.)*

FRASQUITA: Shuffle! Let's read them again!

MERCEDES: *(placing cards on the ground as she speaks)* One . . . two . . . three cards on the right, three on the left. Four go above and four below. Now, we'll see what they foretell for us!

FRASQUITA: *(turning up cards)* Look! I will meet a handsome man who will carry me off on his horse. *(Turns up card.)* And he will become a great leader!

MERCEDES: *(turning cards)* Mine is a wealthy man who will marry me. *(turning another)* I will inherit his fortune when he dies! *(Both laugh, show cards.)*

 11 Underscore—*Carmen's card aria*

CARMEN: *(Kneels.)* I'll deal myself a hand to see what fate holds for me. *(Places cards in formation, begins to turn them up.)* *(speaking in somber tones)* Diamonds! Spades! Death! *(Turns another.)* First I will die, then . . . death for him. *(Looks toward Don José.)* *(Shuffles, speaks as she places cards.)* The cards have spoken—it will not change. *(Turns cards up.)* Again! Again! Death! *(Gathers cards.)* So be it.

Underscore fades here.

(Don José has been assigned to guard the hideout while the smugglers carry out their job. Unseen by José, a fearful but brave Micaela approaches the camp. Just as she recognizes and waves to him, Don José looks in another direction and fires his pistol. Micaela drops to the ground in terror, as Escamillo is seen.)

ESCAMILLO: *(walking toward José, displaying his hat with a bullet hole)* That was a close call!

DON JOSÉ: *(pistol in hand, alert)* Who are you? Give your name!

ESCAMILLO: I am Escamillo, Toreador of Granada.

DON JOSÉ: *(recognizing the famous toreador, returns pistol to holster)* I am honored to meet you. But, why did you take the risk of coming here?

ESCAMILLO: My friend, I am in love with an exciting gypsy woman. The risk is worth it.

DON JOSÉ: Is she a member of the band? What is her name?

ESCAMILLO: Carmen.

DON JOSÉ: *(abruptly)* Carmen? *(slowly, in quiet rage)* Do you know you must pay when you take a gypsy from her people? The price is a duel to the finish.

ESCAMILLO: This toreador welcomes any challenge!

DON JOSÉ: Defend yourself! *(drawing his knife)*

(Escamillo draws his knife; the fight begins. Escamillo slips, falls. Don José is about to strike him. Hearing the shot, Carmen and El Dancairo have returned. Carmen rushes to José, stops him. Other smugglers arrive; they restrain José.)

ESCAMILLO: *(standing, brushing off dirt and bowing to Carmen)* I owe you my life! *(to José)* We will continue this duel whenever you say. *(to all)* I invite you to be my guests at the next bullfight in Seville. *(turns to Carmen)* Those who love me will surely be there. *(Her eyes answer his invitation as he departs.)*

DON JOSÉ: *(still restrained)* I warn you, Carmen, do not push me too far!

SMUGGLER: *(appears, pulling Micaela by her arm)* Look what I've found!

DON JOSÉ: Micaela! *(rushing to her)* What are you doing here?

MICAELA: Please come home to your mother, José. She is so lonely for you, and wants to forgive you. Please.

CARMEN: *(moving toward José)* Well, why don't you leave? You are miserable here. Go on!

DON JOSÉ: *(jealously)* You want me to leave so you can go to Escamillo! *(raging)* No! You belong to me and I will never let you go! Never!

MICAELA: *(interrupting with strength)* José, your <u>mother</u> is <u>dying</u>. Please come now before it is too late!

DON JOSÉ: Dying? *(pause)* I <u>must</u> go to her <u>now</u>! *(Starts to leave with Micaela; turns to Carmen.)* You win this time, but we will meet again. Nothing but death will separate us.

(In the distance, the voice of Escamillo is heard singing the "Toreador Song." Carmen impulsively moves toward the sound. Don José hesitates with a threatening look at Carmen, reconsiders, and moves on as the curtain closes.)

Act IV

THE SCENE: Outside the arena in Seville.

11

March and entrance of Escamillo

NARRATOR: *(over music)* Music heralds the beginning of the bullfight. Toreadors enter in a parade. The crowd's applause changes to cheering as Escamillo appears, accompanied by a radiant Carmen! Frasquita and Mercedes warn Carmen that Don José is in the crowd. She shows no fear. A haggard-looking Don José approaches Carmen, who stands alone.

DON JOSÉ: We meet again!

CARMEN: *(brazenly)* I knew you were here. I was warned to fear for my life, but I have no intention of running from you.

DON JOSÉ: *(sadly, quietly)* I'm here to plead with you, not threaten you. Can we begin again? Forget everything that happened between us.

CARMEN: I have never lied to you. We are finished.

DON JOSÉ: *(imploring)* I must save both of us. I still love you!

CARMEN: *(solemnly)* I knew that one day you would kill me. My love is no longer yours. *(resolutely)* It is over.

DON JOSÉ: You <u>must</u> love me. *(desperately)* Carmen, I will do anything. Please, don't leave me! *(moving toward her)*

CARMEN: *(pushing him away)* Don't try to frighten me! *(boldly)* Free was I born, free will I die! *(Excited shouts are heard from the arena, and the cry of "Victory!" Carmen raises her arms in triumph, moving toward the arena.)*

250

DON JOSÉ: *(blocking Carmen's move, irate)* You will never go to him!
CARMEN: *(struggling)* You cannot stop me! I love him! I love him! *(freeing herself)*
DON JOSÉ: *(furious)* You discard me so you can go to him! Never!
CARMEN: Then kill me! Now! *(cries of "Victory!" "Escamillo!")*
DON JOSÉ: You <u>are</u> a demon!
CARMEN: *(tearing ring from her finger)* Here! *(throwing it, screaming)* Take back the ring you gave me!
DON JOSÉ: *(violently drawing his dagger)* No more! *(She runs; he rushes to overtake her, raging.)* It is finished! *(Stabs her, then falls to his knees beside her body. A triumphant Escamillo, followed by the crowd, emerges; all stop in horror.)*
DON JOSÉ: *(heartbroken)* How I loved you! My beloved Carmen!

THE CURTAIN CLOSES

Follow the score for the last few moments of the original opera.
Don José, desperate for Carmen to return to him, and realizing
that she now loves Escamillo, draws his knife and stabs her to
death. As the crowd leaves the bullring, Don José kneels by
Carmen's lifeless form and sings of his continued adoration of her.
The words are sung in French, but you can follow the English
lyrics underneath. Listen to the way the "fate" motive is used in
this scene.

Duet and Final Chorus (excerpt)

Allegro giocoso

me!
him!

Chorus

Vi - va! Vi - va! la course est bel - le! Vi - va! sur le sa - ble san - glant,
Vi - va! Vi - va! Oh, what a shout-ing! Vi - va! Hail the brave to - re - ro,

Le tau - reau, le tau - reau s'é - lan - ce! Voy - ez, voy - ez, voy - ez, voy -
For the bull is charg-ing and stamp-ing! Oh, look, oh, look, oh, look, oh,

ez!___ Le tau - reau qu'on har - cèle En bon - dis - sant s'é - lan - ce, voy - ez!
look!___ See the bull run-ning head-long, what a great to - re - ro to see!

Moderato Don José

Ain - si, le sa - lut de mon â - me Je l'au - rai per - du pour que
And so, I have for-feit-ed Hea-ven, be - cause I have loved you too

toi, Pour que tu t'en ail - les, in - fâ - me En - tre ses
much, Recit. *With you I've sup-port-ed the wick - ed, And your re -*

a tempo

bras ri - re de moi! Non, par le sang, tu n'ir - as pas! Car - men,
ply has___ been to laugh! No, by my soul, you will not go! Car-men,

Carmen Don José

C'est moi que tu sui - vras! Non, non, ja - mais! Je suis las de te me - na -
You'll come and fol-low me! No, no, I'll not! I am tired of your taunts and

Carmen

cer! Eh bien! Frap - pe - moi donc, ou lais - se - moi pas -
threats! Al - right! Kill me at once, or let me go my

Chorus Don José

ser! Vic - toi - re! Pour la der - niè - re fois, dé - mon, veux - tu me
way! It's o - ver! Now for the fin - al time, you fiend! Will you come

253

The Libretto

You probably know that the word *libretto* means "little book" in Italian. A libretto contains the words of an opera. Librettists—those who write librettos—were considered almost as important as composers during the nineteenth century. Meilhac and Halévy, the librettists for *Carmen,* were sought after by many opera composers because of their skill in writing librettos.

Here is a page of a libretto. The French version is on the left and the English is on the right. The English is a <u>reading</u> translation; it is not meant for singing. The scene is the final scene of the opera—the one you have just heard. How does the English translation compare with the one in the singing score?

DON JOSÉ: Où vas tu?	DON JOSÉ: *Where are you going?*
CARMEN: Laisse-moi!	CARMEN: *Leave me alone!*
DON JOSÉ: Cet homme qu'on acclame, c'est ton nouvel amant!	DON JOSÉ: *This man they are applauding, he's your new sweetheart!*
CARMEN: Laisse-moi! Laisse-moi!	CARMEN: *Leave me alone! Leave me alone!*
DON JOSÉ: Sur mon âme, tu ne passeras pas, Carmen, c'est moi que tu suivras.	DON JOSÉ: *By my soul, you will not pass, Carmen, you will follow me!*
CARMEN: Laisse-moi, Don José, je ne te suivrai pas!	CARMEN: *Leave me alone, Don José, I will not follow you!*
DON JOSÉ: Tu vas le retrouver. Dis, tu l'aimes donc?	DON JOSÉ: *You're going to meet him. Say, you love him then?*
CARMEN: Je l'aime! Je l'aime et devant la mort même, je répèterai que je l'aime!	CARMEN: *I love him! I love him and before death itself I will repeat that I love him!*

The Original Music

You have sung and heard some of the major arias and choruses from *Carmen.* If you wish, you can listen to these selections in their original form. You will find that some of them are longer than the English versions in your book.

 Chorus of Street Boys   *Gypsy Song*

 Habanera   *Toreador Song*

What Do You Hear? 2

10 *Father and Son* .... Stevens

Copy the chart below on a separate sheet of paper. As you listen to
Father and Son again fill in what you think are possible answers.
Remember, sometimes there may be no definite answer. Opinions
about music can vary.

What to Listen for	Father	Son
Pitch (lower or higher)		
Dynamics (softer or louder)		
Tempo (fast, slow, moderate)		
Most important instruments heard (guitar, bass, or drums)		
Mood (relaxed, more tense)		

Test 10 ✓

Circle T if the statement is true. Circle F if the statement is false.

1. A singer's range is the lowest note to the highest note that the singer can sing.

    T   F

2. A *great staff* is a score consisting of two staffs, the top staff in the treble clef, the bottom staff in the bass clef.

    T   F

3. Girls' voices do not change in quality as they mature.

    T   F

4. When tenors read their music in treble clef, their tones sound an octave lower.

    T   F

5. To sing with expression a performer must pay attention to the melody, dynamics, words, range, tempo, and the general mood of the music.

    T   F

Choose the correct answer for these questions.

6. Composers sometimes use phrase lines to show the performer where to breathe. These lines are called _____.
    a. ties   c. slurs
    b. breath marks   d. dynamics

7. Singers prepare to sing by doing a series of _____.
    a. push ups   c. squat thrusts
    b. warm ups   d. chin ups

8. When a score is printed with each voice having its own staff, it is called _____.
    a. closed score   c. voice score
    b. even score   d. open score

9. When a score is printed on only two staffs, two voices on each staff, it is called _____.
    a. closed score   c. voice score
    b. even score   d. open score

10. *A cappella* means _____.
    a. at the chapel   c. sung loudly
    b. unaccompanied   d. sung slowly

Choose the correct answer and write its letter in the blank.

1. Benny Goodman was called _____.
   a. The Sultan of Swat   c. The Thane of Cawdor
   b. The King of Swing   d. Clarinet Man

2. The first show choir was developed by _____.
   a. Duke Ellington   c. Igor Stravinsky
   b. Frank Sinatra   d. Fred Waring

3. "Bye-Bye Blackbird," "Tip-Toe thru the Tulips," and "Button Up Your Overcoat" are songs that were written in _____.
   a. The Roaring Twenties   c. The Fighting Forties
   b. The Thrilling Thirties   d. The Frightful Fifties

4. Two songs that can be sung together, such as "Walkin' Along" and "Me and My Shadow" are called _____.
   a. togetherness songs   c. partner songs
   b. you-and-me songs   d. double songs

5. *The Erlking* is a German art song called a _____.
   a. ballad   c. aria
   b. lied   d. recitative

6. *The Erlking* was composed by an Austrian composer named _____.

   a. Cosmo Moon   c. Franz Schubert
   b. Arnold Schoenberg   d. Jean Sibelius

7. A Baroque-period English composer who wrote much vocal music, including the opera *Dido and Aeneas*, is _____.
   a. Philip Glass   c. Carmino Ravosa
   b. Aaron Copland   d. Henry Purcell

8. A piece written to celebrate the birthday of Queen Mary was _____.

   a. *In C*   c. "Sound the Trumpet"
   b. *Clair de lune*   d. "Hallelujah" Chorus

9. A kind of "speech-song" used by singers is called _____.
   a. recitative   c. solo
   b. aria   d. chorus

10. A kind of song in opera in which the action of the opera stops is the _____.
    a. aria   c. interlude
    b. recitative   d. prelude

Test 12 ✓

Write T in the blank if the statement is true. Write F if the statement is false.

1. In the opera *Carmen,* the character of Micaela is a young girl from Don José's village.

T   F

2. The aria *Habanera* is sung by Don José.

T   F

3. At the beginning of Act II of *Carmen,* a "Gypsy Song" is sung by Escamillo, the toreador.

T   F

4. Don José sings an aria to Carmen called "The Flower Song."

T   F

5. Act II of *Carmen* closes with Don José joining the smugglers.

T   F

Choose your answers to these questions and write their letters in the blanks.

6. In Act III Don José decides to leave the smugglers' den because _____.
   - a. he hates Carmen
   - b. Escamillo tells him to go
   - c. he wants to go back to the army
   - d. his mother is ill

7. As Escamillo leaves, he can be heard singing _____.
   - a. "The Toreador Song"
   - b. "Ferdinand the Bull"
   - c. "Toro, Toro, Toro"
   - d. "The Gypsy Song"

8. In Act IV Carmen is met in the plaza by _____, who has come to try to win her back.
   - a. Escamillo
   - b. Lillas Pastia
   - c. Don José
   - d. Zuniga

9. Carmen, refusing to be "owned," shouts _____.
   - a. "It don't mean a thing if it ain't got that swing."
   - b. "Free was I born, free will I die."
   - c. "Give me liberty, or give me death."

10. In showing Don José she is really finished with him, she _____.
   - a. throws his ring at him
   - b. kicks him
   - c. slaps him
   - d. tells him she's really his long-lost sister

America

Words by Samuel Francis Smith   Music by Henry Carey

Applaud for Us

Words and Music by Steven L. Rosenhaus

Slowly, freely

We've sung our songs and har-mo-nized, and now we'll give it one more try to

We've sung our songs and har-mo-nized, and now we'll give it one more try to

We've sung our songs and har-mo-nized, and now we'll give it one more try to

We've sung our songs and har-mo-nized, and now we'll give it one more try to

en-ter-tain and help to make you smile._____ We hope that you____ en-

en-ter-tain and help to make you smile._____ We hope that you____ en-

en-ter-tain and help to make you smile._____

en-ter-tain and help to make you smile._____

264

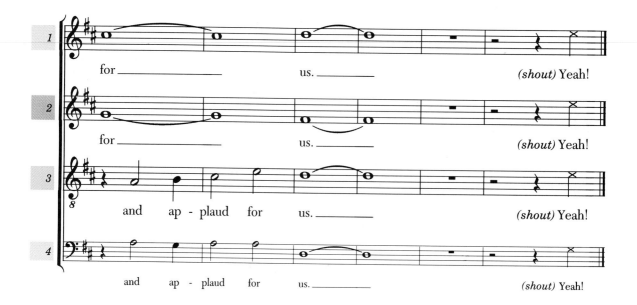

1 for _____ us. _____ *(shout)* Yeah!

2 for _____ us. _____ *(shout)* Yeah!

3 and ap - plaud for us. _____ *(shout)* Yeah!

4 and ap - plaud for us. _____ *(shout)* Yeah!

Autumn Song

Words and Music by Barberi Paull

Now an au-tumn day, now an-oth-er sea-son is in the winds that whis-per

low; Sing - ing us her song, tell - ing us the rea - sons

which hide in times that come and times that go. _____ And how the

leaves change their col-or and come tum-bling, tum-bling down; The winds grow cold-er and

blow a-round_and a - round (a-round_ and a - round) and leaves_tum-ble down. _____

Now the sky is dark ear - ly in the ev-'ning; A day a - go the sky was

A Balm in Gilead

Black Spiritual

REFRAIN

There — is a balm in Gil-e-ad To make the wound-ed whole; —

There — is a balm in Gil-e-ad To make the wound-ed whole; —

There — is a balm in Gil-e-ad To heal the sin-sick soul.

There — is a balm in Gil-e-ad To heal the sin-sick soul.

Brazilian Samba

Words by Richard Eisman and Edward Smaldone   Music by Edward Smaldone

With a Latin swing

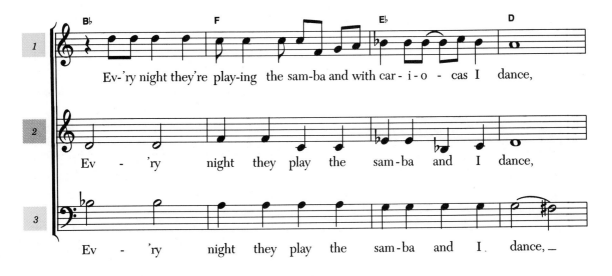

Ev-'ry night they're play-ing the sam-ba and with car - i - o - cas I dance,

Ev - 'ry night they play the sam-ba and I dance,

Ev - 'ry night they play the sam-ba and I dance, —

(No maracas, claves, bells)

In the streets of trop-i-cal Ri - o, I may find Bra-zil - ian ro - mance!

In the streets of Ri - o, I may find ro - mance!

In the streets of Ri - o, find Bra-zil - ian ro - mance!

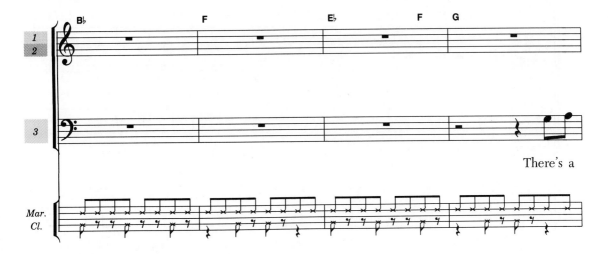

There's a

Mar.
Cl.

Break Forth, O Beauteous Heav'nly Light

Johann Schop   Arranged by Theron Haithwaite, after J. S. Bach

Cielito lindo

Folk Song from Mexico   English Version by Samuele Maquí

1. E - se lu - nar que tie - nes, Cie - li - to
eh - seh loo - nahr keh tyeh - nehs syeh - lee - toh
Night and day 'neath your win - dow, Cie - li - to

lin - do, Jun - to a la bo - ca,
leen - doh hoon - toh ah lah boh - kah
lin - do, play - ing and sing - ing.

No se lo des a na - die, Cie - li - to
noh seh loh dehs ah nah - dyeh syeh - lee - toh
My gui - tar strum - ming from a - far brings my

lin - do, Que a mi me to - ca.
leen - doh keh ah mee meh toh - kah
song to you soft - ly wing - ing.

279

¡Ay — ay, ay, ay! _____ Can - ta_y no
kahn - tah_ee noh
Hush, now your

llo - res _____ Por - que can - tan - do se_a - le - gran, Cie -
yoh - rehs pohr - keh kahn - tahn - doh seh_ah - leh - grahn syeh -
weep - ing; _____ We'll sing, we'll dance at our wed - ding, Cie -

- li - to lin - do, Los _____ co - ra - zo - nes. _____
- lee - toh leen - doh lohs koh - rah - soh - nehs
- li - to lin - do, hap - py to - geth - er. _____

2. Si tu ma-má te di-ce,   see too mah-mah teh dee-seh   *If your mother should tell you,*
   Cie-li-to lin-do,   syeh-lee-toh leen-doh   *Cielito lindo,*
      "Cie-rra la puer-ta,"   syeh-rah lah pwehr-tah   *"Come from your window,"*
   Ha-ce rui-do a la lla-ve,   ah-seh rwee-doh ah lah yah-veh   *I'll await by the garden gate,*
   Cie-li-to lin-do, Y   syeh-lee-toh leen-doh ee   *You're my fate,*
      de-ja-la a-bier-ta.   deh-hah-lah ah-byehr-tah   *my Cielito lindo.*

The Cold December
(El desembre congelat)

Traditional Catalonian Carol   Arranged by Mary E. Hoffman

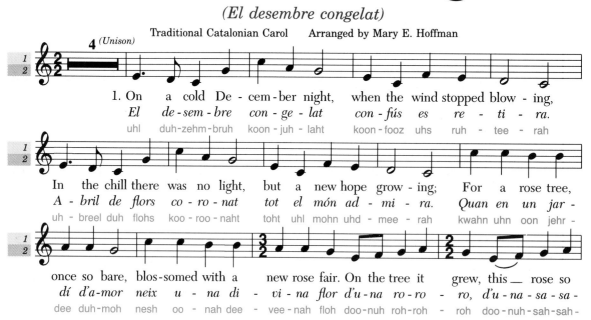

1. On a cold De - cem - ber night, when the wind stopped blow - ing,
El de - sem - bre con - ge - lat con - fús es re - ti - ra.
uhl duh-zehm-bruh koon - juh - laht koon-fooz uhs ruh - tee - rah

In the chill there was no light, but a new hope grow - ing; For a rose tree,
A - bril de flors co - ro - nat tot el món ad - mi - ra. Quan en un jar -
uh - breel duh flohs koo - roo - naht toht uhl mohn uhd - mee - rah kwahn uhn oon jehr -

once so bare, blos-somed with a new rose fair. On the tree it grew, this _ rose so
dí d'a-mor neix u - na di - vi - na flor d'u - na ro - ro - ro, d'u - na - sa - sa -
dee duh-moh nesh oo - nah dee - vee-nah floh doo-nuh roh-roh - roh doo-nuh-sah-sah-

star, the star beam glow - ing, bright - ness ev - er grow - ing.
sol, d'u - na bel - la au - ro - ra que el cel en - a - mor - a.
sohl doo - nuh bay - lyah ow - roh - ruh kuh ehl sehl uhn - uh - moh - ruh

star, the star beam glow - ing, bright - ness ev - er grow - ing.
la, d'u - na bel - la au - ro - ra que el cel en - a - mor - a.
lah doo - nuh bay - lyah ow - roh - ruh kuh ehl sehl uhn - uh - moh - ruh

Come Away 🎵

(Ven acá, muchacha)

Words and Music by Juan F. Garcia   English Version by Samuele Maqui

Come a - way, my pret - ty one, now come a - way; You and
Ven a - cá, cie - li - to lin - do, ven a - cá; tú y yo
vehn ah - kah cyeh - lee - toh leen - doh vehn ah - kah too ee yoh

I to - geth - er we must roam. Come a - way, my pret - ty one, now
so - los de - be - mos es - tar. Ven a - cá, cie - li - to lin - do,
soh - lohs deh - beh - mohs ehs - tahr vehn ah - kah cyeh - lee - toh leen - doh

come a - way, come a - way, we'll wan - der far from home. We will
ven a - cá, ven a o - ír lo que te quie - ro ha - blar. No te a -
vehn ah - kah vehn ah oh - eer loh keh teh kyeh - roh ah - blahr noh teh ah -

nev - er be un - hap - py, no, no, no; I'll pro - tect you all my
sus - tes, mi vi - di - ta, no, no, no; na - da ma - lo te pue - de pa -
soos - tehs mee vee - dee - tah noh noh noh nah - dah mah - loh teh pweh - deh pah -

life._____ An-swer now this ques-tion that I ask of you:_____ Will you
sar._____ *Lo que yo quie-ro de-cir-te o-ye-lo*_____ *que con-*
sahr   loh keh yoh kyeh - roh deh-seer-teh oh - yeh-loh   keh kohn -

mar - ry me and be my wife?_____ Come a - wife?_____ Come a -
*ti - go me quie-ro ca-sar.*_____ *Ven a - sar.*_____ *Ven a -*
tee - goh meh kyeh - roh kah - sahr   vehn ah - sahr   vehn ah -

way, *mu - cha - cha,*_____ come a - way._____ Come and hear me whis - per -
*cá, mu - cha - cha,*_____ *ven a - cá,*_____ *Ven que quie-ro ha-blar - te,* __
kah moo - chah - chah   vehn ah - kah   vehn keh eg -roh ah- blahr - teh

__ "Come a - way."____ Come a - way, *mu - cha - cha,* why such hes - i - tat - ing?___
__ *ven a - cá.*_____ *Ven a - cá, mu - cha - cha, no seas ci - ma - rro - na,*__
vehn ah - kah   vehn ah - kah moo-chah - chah noh sehahs see-mah - rroh - nah

__ Can't you see that you're_ the one that I'm a - wait - ing?_____ Come a -
__ *mi - ra que te quie - ro con ve - lo y co - ro - na.*_____ *Ven a -*
mee - rah keh teh kyeh - roh kohn veh-loh ee koh - roh - nah   vehn ah -

wait - ing?_____ Come a - way, *mu - cha - cha,*__ come a - way._____ Come a -
*ro - na.*_____ *Ven a - cá, mu - cha - cha,*__ *ven a - cá.*_____ *Ven a -*
roh - nah   vehn ah - kah moo - chah - chah   vehn ah - kah   vehn ah -

way, *mu - cha - cha,*_____ come a - way._____
*cá, mu - cha - cha,*_____ *ven a - cá.*_____
kah moo - chah - chah   vehn ah - kah

Come Sigh with Me ⑫

(Venid a suspirar)

Anonymous Song from Spain English Words by Samuele Maquí

(Musical score, three vocal parts)

Part 1:
Come sigh, come sigh with me in the green mead - ow, in the green
Ve - nid a sus - pi - rar al ver - de pra - do, al ver - de
veh - need ah soohs-pee-rahr ahl vehr-deh prah - doh ahl vehr - deh

Part 2:
Come sigh, come sigh with me in the green mead - ow, in the green ___
Ve - nid a sus - pi - rar al ver - de pra - do, al ver - de ___

Part 3:
Come sigh, come sigh with me in the green mead - ow, in the green
Ve - nid a sus - pi - rar al ver - de pra - do, al ver - de

Part 1:
mead - ow. Come sigh with me, my young friends, ___ come sigh with me, my young ___
pra - do. Co - mi - go, za - ga - le - jos, ___ co - mi - go, za - ga - le -
prah - doh koh - mee - goh sah-gah-leh - hohs koh - mee-goh sah - gah - leh-

Part 2:
___ mead-ow. Come sigh with me, my young friends, come sigh with
___ pra - do. Co - mi - go, za - ga - le - jos, Co - mi - go,

Part 3:
mead - ow. Come sigh with me, my young friends, come sigh with me, my
pra - do. Co - mi - go, za - ga - le - jos, co - mi - go, za - ga -

Part 1:
___ friends, and all you shep - herds. I die, and yet I live, I
- jos, y vos pas - to - res. Pues mue - ro sin mo - rir, mue -
- hohs ee vohs pahs-toh - rehs pwehs mweh-roh seen moh-reer mweh-

Part 2:
me, my young friends, and all you shep-herds. I die, and yet I live, I
za - ga - le - jos, y vos pas - to - res. Pues mue - ro sin mo - rir, mue -

Part 3:
young friends, and all you shep - herds. I die, and yet I live, I
le - jos, y vos pas - to - res. Pues mue - ro sin mo - rir, mue -

284

die, yet I live; I die of love's pain, I die ___ of love's pain.
ro sin mo - rir, de mal de̤a - mo - res, de mal ___ de̤a - mo - res.
roh seen moh - reer deh mahl deh̤ah - moh - rehs deh mahl deh̤ah - moh - rehs

die, yet I live; I die of love's pain, I die ___ of love's pain.
ro sin mo - rir, de mal de̤a - mo - res, de mal ___ de̤a - mo - res.

die, yet I live; I die of love's pain, I die of love's ___ pain.
ro sin mo - rir, de mal de̤a - mo - res, de mal de̤a - mo - res.

Cool Water

Words and Music by Bob Nolan   Arranged by Lawrence Eisman

1. All day I've faced a bar - ren waste with - out the taste of wa - ter,
nights are cool and I'm a fool, each star's a pool of wa - ter,

(few voices)
wa - ter, wa - ter
Cool ___ wa - ter. _____

Old Dan and I with throats burnt dry and
But with the dawn I'll wake and yawn, and

(Melody)

wa - ter, wa - ter
(Melody) wa - ter
souls that cry for wa - ter, _____ Cool,
car - ry on to wa - ter, _____

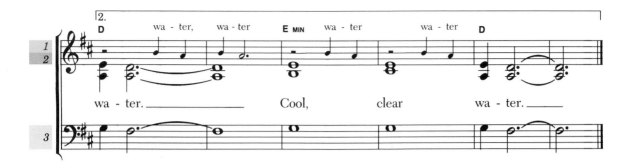

wa - ter. _____ Cool, clear wa - ter. _____

Dona Nobis

Words Traditional   Music by Sol Berkowitz

Do - na no - bis pa - cem,

Do - na no - bis pa - cem,

Do - na no - bis pa - cem, pa - cem,

Do - na no - bis pa - cem,

pa - cem, pa - cem, pa - cem. _____

Do - na no - bis pa - cem,

Do - na no - bis pa - cem,   Do - na no - bis

Do - na no - bis,   do - na no - bis,   do - na no - bis, do - na

no - bis, do - na no - bis pa - cem,   pa - cem,   pa -   cem. ____

Irish workers who first came to this country were called "terriers"
because their stubby red beards looked like terriers' coats.
The word *tarrier* is an Irish adaptation of terrier.

Drill, Ye Tarriers

Words and Music by Thomas Casey   Arranged by Linda Williams

1. Ev - 'ry morn - in' at sev - en o' clock there's twen - ty tar - ri - ers a -
2. Our new fore - man is Dan ___ Mc - Cann, I'll tell you sure ___ he's a
3. Next time pay - day comes ___ a - round, Jim Goff was short ___ one ___

1. Drill,   ye   tar - ri - ers, drill, "And ___
2. Drill,   ye   tar - ri - ers, drill, And a
3. Drill,   ye   tar - ri - ers, drill, "You're ___

work - in' at the rock, And the boss comes a - long and he says, "Keep still, and
blame ___ mean ___ man; Last ___ week a ___ pre ma - ture ___ blast went off, And a
buck, ___ he ___ found; "What ___ for?" says ___ he; then ___ this re - ply, "You're

*Treble voices may sing the baritone part an octave higher.

290

This added part may be repeated throughout the refrain.

Drill, ye tar-ri-ers, drill.

Green Grow the Lilacs

American Folk Song   Arranged by Lawrence Eisman

He's Gone Away

American Folk Song   Arranged by Mary E. Hoffman

mp

1. He's gone a-way ___ for to stay a lit-tle while, But he's

com-in' back, ___ tho' he go ten thou-sand miles. Oh, who will tie my

shoes? And who will glove my hands? And who will kiss ___ my ru-by lips

rit.   *a tempo*

when he is gone? Look a-way, look a-way o-ver

Yan-dro.   Part 2   *mf*   2. I'm goin' a-way ___

___ for to stay a lit-tle while, But I'm com-in' back, ___

___ tho' I go ten thou-sand miles. Oh, dad-dy will tie your

f

And mom-my will glove my hands, And you will kiss ___

f

shoes.   And I will kiss ___

my ru - by lips.

your ru - by lips when I re - turn. Look a -

Look a - way, _____ look a - way _____ o - ver Yan - dro.

way, look a - way, look a - way o - ver Yan - dro.

Hwi Ne Ya He 12

American Indian Song

♩ = 88
Voices

Hwi ne ya he ya he ya ho hwi ne ya he yo
hwee neh yah heh yah heh yah hoh

Bells (unpitched), Drum

hwi ne ya he ya ho hwi ne ya he yo hwi ne ya he yo

Bls., Dr.

hwi ne ya he ya ho ya he ya ho we ya he he e

Bls., Dr.

Japanese Lullaby 🄬

Folk Song from Japan   Arranged by Bruce Saylor

295

Translation:

The baby looks sweet when asleep; (it) looks unpleasant when awake and crying. Today is the 25th day; tomorrow we will go to the shrine for the baby. When you go to the shrine, what will you pray for? That this baby should live in good health throughout its life.

The *John B.* Sails

Folk Song from the Bahama Islands
Arranged by Raymond J. Malone and Mary E. Hoffman

sights, _____ Well, I feel so break_ up, _ I want_ to go home.
home, _____ Well, I feel so break_ up, _ I want_ to go home.
home, _____ Well, this is the worst_ trip_ since I _____ was born.

REFRAIN

So, hoist up _ the *John B.* sails, See how _ the main-s'l set,

Send for _ the Cap-t'n a - shore, Let _ me go home. Please let _ me go

home, I want _ to go home. _____ Well,_ I

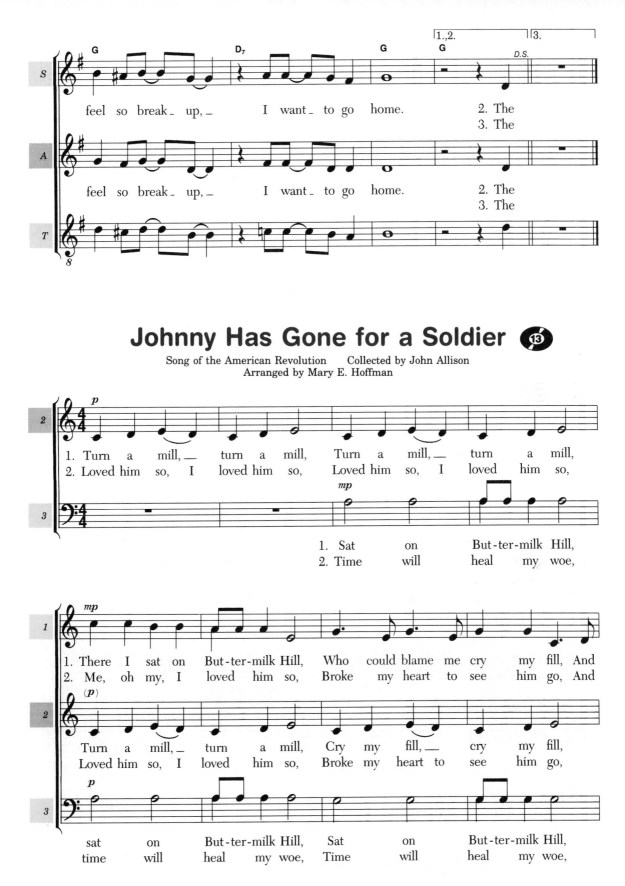

Johnny Has Gone for a Soldier

Song of the American Revolution   Collected by John Allison
Arranged by Mary E. Hoffman

ev - 'ry drop would turn a mill;
on - ly time will heal my woe; John-ny has gone for a sol - dier.

Ev - 'ry drop would turn a mill;
On - ly time will heal my woe; John-ny has gone for a sol - dier.

sat on But-ter-milk Hill;
time will heal my woe; John-ny has gone for a sol - dier.

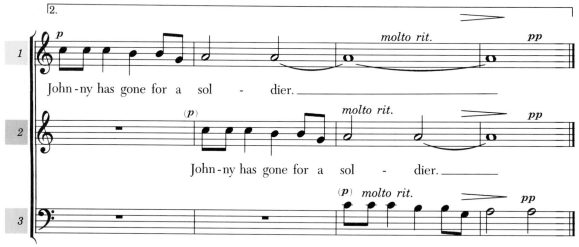

John-ny has gone for a sol - dier.

John-ny has gone for a sol - dier.

John-ny has gone for a sol - dier.

Just a Vo-dee-oh-do 🔟

Words and Music by Raymond Granito

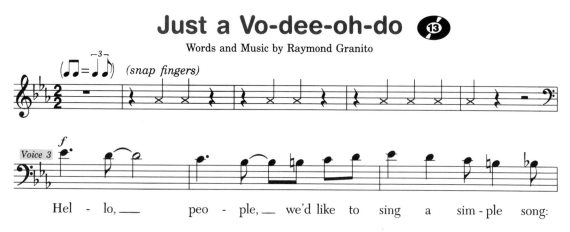

Voice 3

Hel - lo, peo - ple, we'd like to sing a sim - ple song:

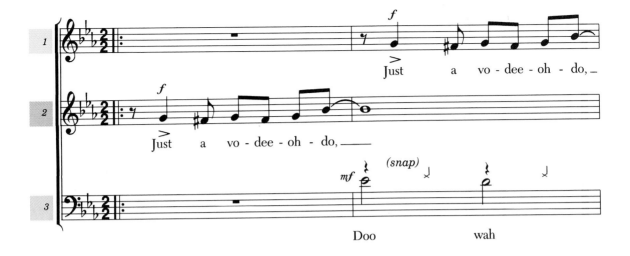

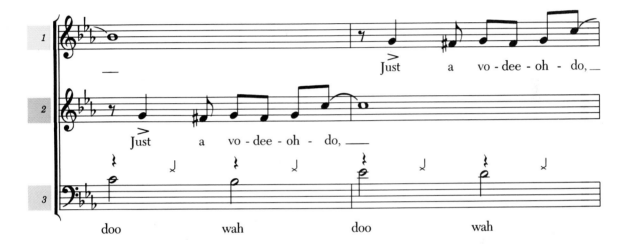

Line 1:
hands   a-clap-pin' with me.____   You'll find that
smile   a-wait-in' for me.____   You'll start to
rain-bow's love-ly to see.____   You'll feel your

Line 2:
hands   a-clap-pin' with me.____
smile   a-wait-in' for me.____
rain-bow's love-ly to see.____

Line 3:
doo   wah
Just   a-clap-pin' with me.
Smile   a-wait-in' for me.
Rain-bow's love-ly to see.

Line 1:
you'll be feel-ing bet-ter ev-'ry time you sing the song,   So o-pen
be more un-der-stand-ing, you will al-ways fig-ure out   that it's no
feet be-gin a-tap-pin', and your bod-y start to sway;   You'll no-tice

Line 2:
oo____   oo____

Line 3:
oo____

Line 1:
up your heart and sing____ it, you can nev-er, ev-er go wrong.
use to cry and wor-ry, sing-in' this-'ll help you____ out.
all your trou-bles leav-in', Jan-u-a-ry turns to____ May.

Line 2:
oo____   nev-er   wrong.
help   you   out.
turns   to   May.

Line 3:
oo____   nev-er   wrong.
help   you   out.
turns   to   May.

303

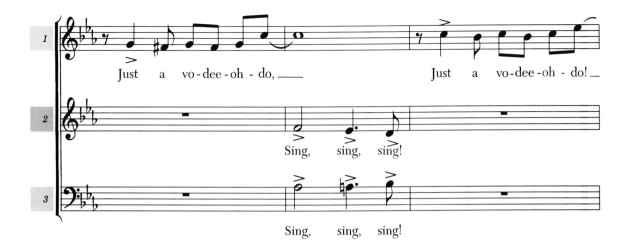

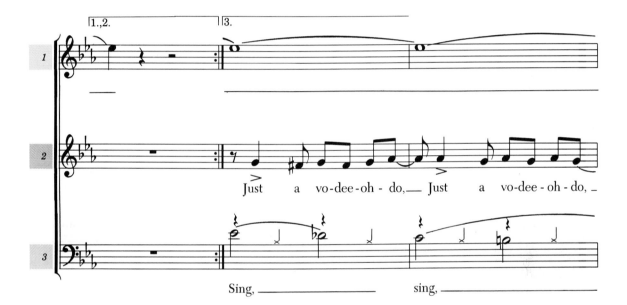

Keep the Dream Alive

Words and Music by Reggie Harris

Well, it's the way of ___ the world ___ to keep on ___ mov - in'; ___ Yes, it's the way of ___ the world ___ to keep mov - in' on ___ and ___ on; But now the time has ___ be - gun, ___ we must put it all ___ to - geth - er; ___

If we work hand ___ in hand, ___ we can all live as one.

Oh, ___ the world needs ___ your love ___ and the world ___ needs just what
way of ___ all life, we've got to try ___ to help each

you pos - sess; ___ For the wealth of ___ us all ___
oth - er. ___ If you give of ___ your - self ___

___ is in the fam - 'ly of love. So, come on ___ and
___ you will re - ceive in re - turn, And ___ then that

shine ___ your light, just shine it out ___ right through the dark - ness; ___
spir - it ___ will grow to all your sis - ters and your broth - ers. ___

And then the fu-ture___ will be _____ bright-er for us

Now we've got so much___ to share, _____ lots of things to

all.

learn. Try to re-mem-ber that

Ev-'ry lit-tle bit you can

do makes it bet - ter; ___ Ev-'ry good thing you can

say makes it work; Ev-'ry lit-tle smile ___ makes

some-bod - y hap - py; ___ We've got to keep the dream ___ a - live!

(a few voices)

(All)

D.S. al Fine

Keep the dream a - live. _____ Well, it's the

Light the Candle ⑬

Words and Music by David Eddleman

Unison

mp

Light the can - dle, spin the drey - dl, what ___ a mer - ry sight to see;

Eight full days of cel - e - bra - tion for ___ the mir - a - cle of old,

For these days are hol - i - days, the fes - ti - val of Mac - ca - bee.

For the He - brew vic - to - ry and for ___ the sto - ry that was told.

f

Hey, ho, and light the can - dle, sing a song and spin the top;

How the me - nor - ah flick - ers, drey - dl nev - er seems to stop.

mf

Let us sing a song of glee, Joy - ous
Ha - nuk - kah has come once more; Cel - e -

time that comes to be; See the me - nor - ah's light,
brate those days of yore, When Mac - ca - bee won the fight, The

1.

Shin - ing oh, so bright.
lamp burned eight full nights.

2. *accelerando*

much faster

f

1. Light the can - dle, spin the drey - dl, what a mer - ry sight to see;
Eight full days of cel - e - bra - tion for the mir - a - cle of old,

2. *f*

Let us sing a song of glee,
Ha - nuk - kah has come once more;

1. For these days are hol - i - days, the fes - ti - val of Mac - ca - bee.
For the He - brew vic - to - ry and for the sto - ry that was told.

2. Joy - ous time that comes to be;
Cel - e - brate those days of yore,

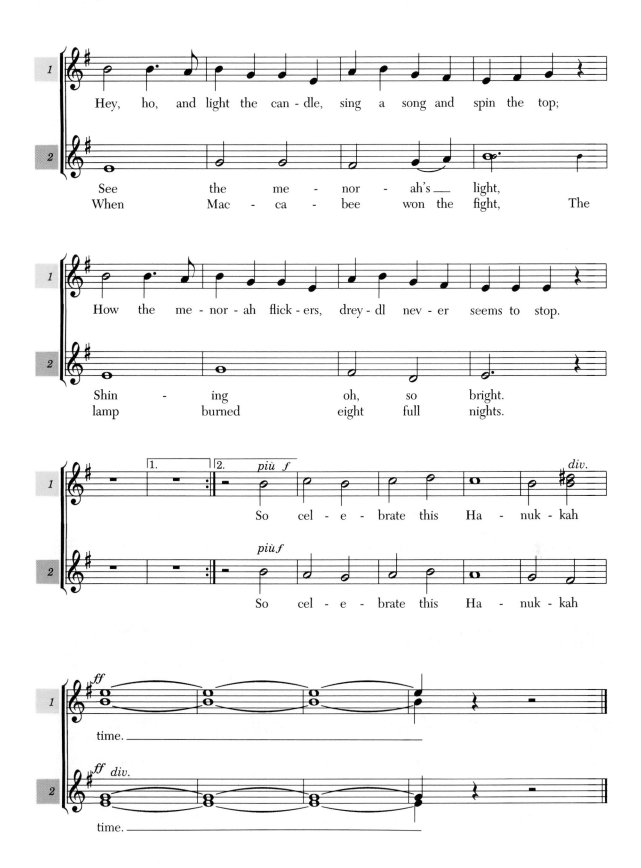

My Cherie Amour

Words and Music by Stevie Wonder, Henry Cosby, and Sylvia Moy
Arranged by Linda Williams

How I wish that you were mine. _____ La la la la ___ la

How I wish that you were mine. _____ La la la la ___ la

How I wish that you were mine. _____ La la la la ___ la

la, La la la la ___ la la. May - be some __ day __ you'll

la, La la la la ___ la la. May - be some __ day __ you'll

la, La la la la ___ la la. May - be

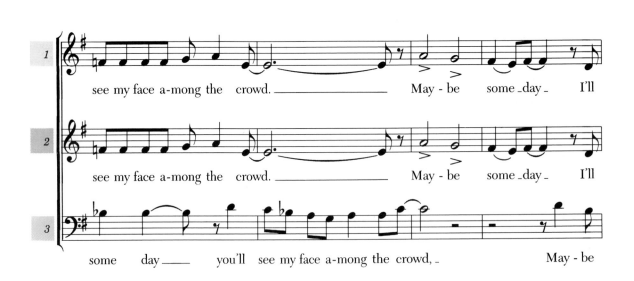

see my face a-mong the crowd. _____ May - be some __ day __ I'll

see my face a-mong the crowd. _____ May - be some __ day __ I'll

some day ___ you'll see my face a-mong the crowd, __ May - be

My Lord, What a Mornin'

Black Spiritual   Arranged by Alan Seale

la la la la. La la la.

la la la la. La la la.

la la la la. La la la.

My Lord, what a morn-in', My Lord, what a morn-in',

My Lord, what a morn-in', Oh, my Lord, what a morn-in',

My Lord, what a morn-in', When the stars be-gin to fall.

My Lord, what a morn-in', When the stars be-gin to fall.

1. You'll
2. You'll
3. You'll

hear the trum-pet sound
hear the sin-ner cry
hear the faith-ful shout
to wake the na-tions un-der-ground.

Now the Day Is Over

Words and Music by S. Baring-Gould and Joseph Barnby   Arranged by Lawrence Eisman

1. Now the day is o - ver, Night is draw-ing nigh,
2. When the morn-ing wak - ens, Then may I a - rise

1. Now the day is o - ver, Night is draw-ing nigh,
2. When the morn - ing wak - ens, Then may I a - rise

1. Now the day is o - ver, Night is draw-ing nigh,
2. When the morn-ing wak - ens, Then may I a - rise

Shad - ows of the eve - ning Steal a-cross the sky.
Pure and fresh and sin - less In Thy ho - ly eyes.

Shad - ows of the eve - ning Steal a-cross the sky.
Pure and fresh and sin - less In Thy ho - ly eyes.

Shad - ows of the eve - ning Steal a-cross the sky.
Pure and fresh and sin - less In Thy ho - ly eyes.

Look-in' to my God's right hand, When the stars be-gin to fall.

Look-in' to my God's right hand, When the stars be-gin to fall.

Partners in Minor

(Zum Gali Gali/Shalom, Chaverim/Annie, The Miller's Daughter)

Arranged by Mary E. Hoffman

ZUM GALI GALI
Folk Song from Israel

Zum ga - li ga - li, ga - li, Zum ga - li ga - li,
zoom gah - lee gah - lee gah - lee

Zum ga - li ga - li, ga - li, Zum ga - li ga - li.   °He - cha - lutz   l' -
hay - khah - loots   luh -

(Part 2)

man a - vo - dah;   A - vo - dah l' - man he - cha - lutz.
mahn ah - voh - dah   ah - voh - dah luh - mahn hay - khah - loots

SHALOM, CHAVERIM Folk Song from Israel

**Sha - lom, cha - ver - im! Sha - lom, cha - ver - im! Sha - lom, sha - lom!   L' -
shah - lohm khah - vehr - eem shah - lohm khah - vehr - eem shah - lohm shah - lohm   luh -

(Parts 2 and 3)

hit - ra - ot, l' - hit - ra - ot, Sha - lom,   sha - lom.
heet - rah - oht luh - heet - rah - oht shah - lohm   shah - lohm

Sha - lom, cha - ver - im!   Sha - lom, cha - ver - im! Sha -

Zum ga - li ga - li, ga - li, Zum ga - li ga - li,

°The pioneer's purpose is labor;
Labor is for the pioneer.

**Goodbye (or peace), friends,
Until we meet again.

lom,   sha - lom!   L' - hit - ra - ot, l' -

Zum ga - li ga - li, ga - li, Zum ga - li ga - li.   He - cha - lutz l' -

hit - ra - ot, Sha - lom,   sha - lom.

man a - vo - dah;   A - vo - dah l' - man he - cha - lutz.

mf **ANNIE, THE MILLER'S DAUGHTER**
Folk Song from Czechoslovakia

An - nie,   An - nie   was the mil - ler's daugh - ter,

mp

Sha - lom, cha - ver - im! Sha - lom, cha - ver - im! Sha -

Zum ga - li ga - li, ga - li, Zum   ga - li ga - li,

far she wan - dered   by the sing - ing wa - ter. I - dle,   i - dle

mf   *f*

lom,   sha - lom!   L' - hit - ra - ot, l' -

f

Zum ga - li ga - li, ga - li, Zum   ga - li ga - li.   He - cha - lutz l' -

An-nie went a-may-ing, Up-hill, down-hill, went her flock a-stray-ing.

hit - ra - ot, Sha - lom, sha - lom. Sha -

man a - vo-dah; A - vo-dah l' - man he-cha-lutz.

Hear them, hear them, call-ing as they roam. An - nie, An - nie,

lom, sha - lom. Sha - lom, sha -

Zum ga - li ga - li, ga - li, Zum ga - li ga - li, Zum ga - li ga - li, ga - li,

bring your white sheep home. An - nie, An - nie, bring your white sheep home.

lom.

Zum ga - li ga - li, ga - li.

Slowly

rit.

Bring your white sheep home; bring your white sheep home.

mp *rit.*

Sha-lom, sha-lom.

mp *rit.*

Zum ga-li ga-li, ga-li, Zum.

Raindrops Keep Fallin' on My Head

Words by Hal David Music by Burt Bacharach Arranged by Linda Williams

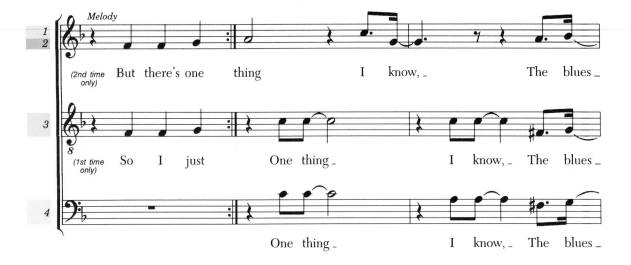

(2nd time only) But there's one thing   I know, ___   The blues ___

(1st time only) So   I   just   One thing ___   I   know, ___   The blues ___

One   thing ___   I   know, ___   The blues ___

___ they   send ___   to   meet ___ me   won't   de - feat ___   me; ___   *Melody*

___ they   send ___   to   meet ___ me   won't   de - feat ___   me; ___   It

___ they   send ___   to   meet ___ me   won't   de - feat ___   me; ___

Hap - pi - ness   steps up ___ to greet _ me. ___

won't be long ___ till hap - pi - ness ___ steps up ___ to greet _ me. ___

Hap - pi - ness   steps up ___ to greet _ me. ___

The Road to Peace

Words by Barbara E. Miller   Music by Gary William Friedman
Countermelody by Claudia Friedlander

We have miles to go down that road to peace, We have miles to go before we reach A place where life is for all to en-joy, For ev-'ry man and wo-man, girl and boy.

Countermelody

We have miles to go down that road to peace, We have miles to go be-

Melody

We have miles to go down that road to peace, We have miles to go be-

fore we reach A time when there's hope for ev-'ry-one To

fore we reach A time when there's hope for ev-'ry-one To

find, find a place un-der the sun.

find a place un-der the sun.

Take the hand of your broth-er and make him your friend; Take the hand of an-oth-er and

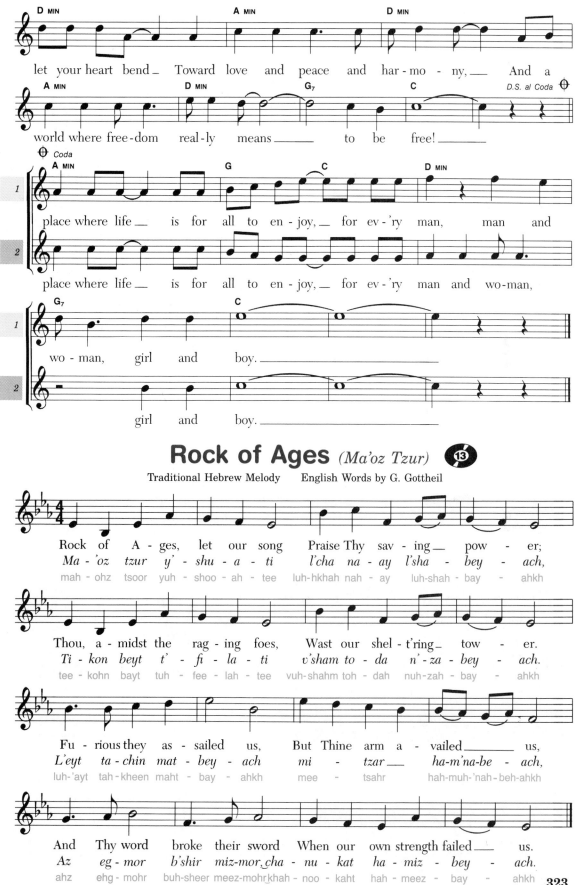

Rock of Ages *(Ma'oz Tzur)*

Traditional Hebrew Melody   English Words by G. Gottheil

Rock of A - ges, let our song   Praise Thy sav - ing__ pow - er;
Ma - 'oz tzur y' - shu - a - ti   l'cha na - ay l'sha - bey - ach,
mah - ohz tsoor yuh - shoo - ah - tee luh-hkhah nah - ay luh-shah - bay - ahkh

Thou, a - midst the rag - ing foes,   Wast our shel - t'ring__ tow - er.
Ti - kon beyt t' - fi - la - ti   v'sham to - da n' - za - bey - ach.
tee - kohn bayt tuh - fee - lah - tee vuh-shahm toh - dah nuh-zah - bay - ahkh

Fu - rious they as - sailed us,   But Thine arm a - vailed_____ us,
L'eyt ta - chin mat - bey - ach   mi - tzar__ ha - m'na - be - ach,
luh-'ayt tah - kheen maht - bay - ahkh mee - tsahr hah-muh-'nah-beh-ahkh

And Thy word broke their sword   When our own strength failed__ us.
Az eg - mor b'shir miz - mor, cha - nu - kat ha - miz - bey - ach.
ahz ehg - mohr buh-sheer meez-mohr khah - noo - kaht hah - meez - bay - ahkh

323

Say Good-by to These Islands *(Ku'u Ipo Ika He'e Pueone)*

Hawaiian Words and Music by Princess Likelike*   English Words by Nickie Hines and David Lahaina

(pronounced LEE keh LEE keh)

So, my good friend, say good-by to all these is - lands,
Ku-'u i - po, i - ka he - 'e pu - e - o - ne,
koo-'oo ee - poh ee-kah heh - 'eh poo-eh - oh - neh

Know your friend-ship will be al - ways in my heart;
I - ke ka - i, ne - he i - ka i - li i - li;
ee - keh kah - ee neh-heh ee - kah ee - lee ee - lee

For it haunts me, and it brings back sweet a - lo - ha,
Ni - po a - ku, i - la - i - lai ka - ma - na - 'o,
nee-poh ah - koo ee-lah - ee - lahee kah-mah - nah - 'oh

And for - ev - er brings back sweet mem - o - ries.
U - a ki - li o - pu, mau - ai ka - na - he - le.
oo - ah kee - lee oh-poo mah-oo-ahee kah - nah - heh - leh

Time now to grieve a - lone in sad - ness,
E a - la e ma - li - u ma - i,
eh ah - lah eh mah - lee - oo mah - ee

Say "a - lo - ha," un - til we meet a - gain,
E ia, ko a - lo - ha e li - a'e ne - i,
eh ee-yah koh ah - loh - hah eh lee - ah'eh neh - ee

Till my a - lo - ha sings with glad - ness,
Hi - ki mai a - na i - ka po ne - i,
hee - kee mah-ee ah - nah ee-kah poh neh - ee

For I know you'll come back a - gain, my friend.
U - a ki - li o - pu, mau - ai ka - na - he - le.
oo - ah kee - lee oh-poo mah-oo-ahee kah - nah - heh - leh

Silent Night

Words by Joseph Mohr   Music by Franz Gruber

1. Si - lent night, ho - ly night, All is calm,
2. Si - lent night, ho - ly night, Shep - herds quake

all is bright Round yon Vir - gin Moth - er and Child.
at the sight, Glo - ries stream __ from heav - en a - far.

Ho - ly In - fant so ten - der and mild, Sleep in heav - en - ly
Heav'n - ly hosts __ sing "Al - le - lu - ia, Christ the Sav - ior is

peace, _____ Sleep __ in heav - en - ly peace.
born! _____ Christ __ the Sav - ior is born!" _____

Simple Gifts

Shaker Hymn

'Tis the gift to be sim - ple, 'Tis the gift to be free, 'Tis the

gift to come down where we ought to be, And when we find our - selves __ in the

place just __ right, 'Twill __ be in the val - ley of love and de - light.

When true sim - pli - ci - ty is gained, To bow and to bend

we __ shan't be a - shamed, To turn, turn will be our de - light,

Till by turn - ing, turn - ing we come round right.

Standin' in the Need of Prayer

Black Spiritual Arranged by Lawrence Eisman

The Star-Spangled Banner

Words by Francis Scott Key   Music by John Stafford Smith

1. Oh, — say! can you see, by the dawn's ear-ly light, What so
2. On the shore, dim-ly seen through the mists of the deep, Where the

proud-ly we hailed at the twi-light's last gleam-ing, Whose broad
foe's haugh-ty host in dread si-lence re-pos-es, What is

stripes and bright stars, through the per-il-ous fight, O'er the
that which the breeze, o'er the tow-er-ing steep, As it

ram-parts we watched were so gal-lant-ly stream-ing? And the
fit-ful-ly blows, half con-ceals, half dis-clos-es? Now it

327

rock - ets' red glare, the bombs burst - ing in air, Gave
catch - es the gleam of the morn - ing's first beam, In full

proof through the night that our flag was still there. Oh,
glo - ry re - flected now __ shines on the stream; 'Tis the

say, does that __ Star - Span - gled Ban - ner __ yet __ wave __ O'er the
Star - Span - gled __ Ban - ner, oh, long may __ it __ wave __ O'er the

land _____ of the free and the home of the brave.
land _____ of the free and the home of the brave.

Streets of London 🔵14

Words and Music by Ralph McTell   Arranged by Lawrence Eisman and Donald Scafuri

1. Have you seen __ the old man in the closed down mar - ket,
2. Have you seen __ the old girl who __ walks the streets of Lon - don,
3. In the all - night ca - fé at a quarter past e - lev - en,

Kick - ing up the pa - pers with his worn out shoes? __
Dirt __ in her hair __ and her clothes in rags? __
Same __ old man sit - ting there __ on his own, __

328

REFRAIN

329

To the Greenwood Tree

Words Traditional   Music by John Hilton

I

Come fol - low, fol - low, fol - low, fol - low, fol - low, fol - low me!

II

Whith-er shall I fol - low, fol - low, fol - low, Whith-er shall I fol - low, fol - low thee?

III

To the green-wood, to the green-wood, To the green-wood, green - wood tree.

Trail to Mexico

American Cowboy Song

(Sing 2nd time only)

2. 'Twas in the ___ spring -

1. It was in the year ___ of ___ eight - y
2. 'Twas in the ___ spring - time ___ of the

- time ___ of the year ___ I vol - un - teered ___

three ___ that A. J. Stin - son ___ hired ___
year ___ I vol - un - teered ___ to ___ drive the

330

Variations on a Chord Progression

(Blue Moon/Can't Help Lovin' That Man/Stormy Weather)

Arranged by Mary E. Hoffman

CAN'T HELP LOVIN' THAT MAN

Words by Oscar Hammerstein II
Music by Jerome Kern

333

STORMY WEATHER

Words by Ted Koehler
Music by Harold Arlen

Don't know why there's no sun up in the sky, — storm-y weath-er, —

Since my man and I — ain't to-geth-er, —

Keeps rain-in' all the time. —

Fish got-ta swim — and birds got-ta fly, —

Blue moon, — you saw me stand-ing a - lone, —

Don't know

I got-ta love — one man till I die, — Can't help

why there's no sun up in the sky, —

lov - in' that man, — Can't help lov - in' that man, —

Storm-y weath-er, — Storm-y

Blue

Glossary

a cappella (p. 162) A term used to indicate unaccompanied choral singing; "in chapel style."

aria (p. 233) In an opera, oratorio, or cantata, a song for solo voice; often designed to show off the singer's vocal ability.

bar lines (p. 72) The vertical lines on the staff, used to mark off groupings of beats.

canon (p. 48) A form in which a melody begins in one part and then is imitated by other parts in an overlapping fashion. *See* round, catch.

catch (p. 27) An English round of the seventeenth and eighteenth centuries; from the Italian word *caccia,* meaning "chase".

coda (p. 120) A short closing section added at the end of a composition.

development (p. 119) The middle section of the sonata form, in which the themes of the exposition are developed and expanded.

dynamics (p. 8) The loudness and softness of sounds.

ensemble (p. 24) A group of players or singers.

exposition (p. 119) The first section of a composition, in which the subject, or thematic material, is introduced.

form (p. 86) The structure of a composition, determined by the way its musical materials are organized.

great or grand staff (p. 135) A two-staff system with the soprano and alto parts shown in the treble clef and the tenor and baritone parts shown in the bass clef.

harmony (p. 16) A related succession of chords.

imitation (p. 166) Successive restatements of a musical idea in different voices.

improvise (p. 111) To make up music as it is being performed; often used in jazz.

interlude (p. 200) Any kind of music inserted between the verses of a song; also, music between the scenes of a play or an opera.

libretto (p. 225) The text of an opera or oratorio; from the Italian word meaning "little book".

lied (p. 207) A German art song, pronounced *leet*.

major scale (p. 64) An arrangement of eight tones in a scale according to the following intervals, or steps: whole, whole, half, whole, whole, whole, half.

medley (p. 177) A set of songs grouped together for a segment of a concert and sung without interruption.

melody (p. 8) A succession of single tones, with rhythm, forming a recognizable musical idea.

meter (p. 29) The way beats of music are grouped, often in sets of two or in sets of three. The meter signature, or time signature (e.g., $\frac{3}{4}$, $\frac{2}{4}$), tells how many beats are in the group, or measure (top number), and the kind of note that gets one beat (bottom number).

minor scale (p. 66) Several arrangements of eight tones in a scale, such as natural minor (whole, half, whole, whole, half, whole, whole) and melodic minor (upward: whole, half, whole, whole, whole, whole, half; downward: whole, whole, half, whole, whole, half, whole).

minuet (p. 116) A stately French dance of the seventeenth and eighteenth centuries that is often included in the third movement of classical symphonies. It is in AB form and in triple meter.

minuet and trio (p. 118) A form in which the minuet is followed by another AB section called the trio, then by a repetition of the original minuet. *See* minuet.

motive (p. 108) A short musical idea or melodic fragment.

octave (p. 140) The distance of eight steps from one tone to another that has the same letter name. On the staff these steps are shown by the lines and spaces. When two notes are an octave apart, there are eight lines and spaces from one note to the other.

opera (p. 225) A theatrical production combining drama, vocal and orchestral music, costumes, scenery, and sometimes, dance.

oratorio (p. 45) A musical drama for voices and orchestra, usually based on a religious narrative; usually performed without scenery or action.

ostinato (p. 87) A rhythmic or melodic idea that keeps repeating throughout a piece or a section of a piece.

overture (p. 8) An instrumental introduction to an opera, oratorio, or other stage work; the term is sometimes given to an independent orchestral composition. *See* prelude.

phrase (p. 51) A melodic idea that acts as a complete idea, something like a sentence.

polyphony (p. 31) The musical texture consisting of two or more independent melodic lines sounding together.

prelude (p. 8) An instrumental introduction to a musical drama, usually shorter than an overture; also, a short, independent composition. *See* overture.

program music (p. 70) Music that is inspired by an extramusical idea—a person, place, story, scene, and so on.

recapitulation (p. 119) The third section of the sonata form, in which the themes are restated and the entire movement is brought to a close.

recitative (p. 217) A speech-like, declamatory vocal style that carries the conversational passages in an opera or oratorio.

rhythm (p. 88) The combination of sounds and silences in the same or differing lengths.

riff (p. 89) A term used in swing for a repeated, short, strongly rhythmic phrase. *See* ostinato.

rondo (p. 102) A form in which the A section alternates with two contrasting sections, creating a plan of ABACA.

round (p. 27) A form in which a melody begins in one part and then is continually and exactly repeated by other parts in an overlapping fashion. *See* canon, catch.

scale (p. 64) An arrangement of pitches from lower to higher according to a specific pattern of intervals. Major, minor, pentatonic, whole-tone, and chromatic are five kinds of scales. Each one has its own arrangement of pitches.

score (p. 159) The musical notation of a composition, showing all vocal and instrumental parts. *See* system.

sonata-allegro (p. 119) A general musical form consisting of three major divisions: the *exposition,* in which themes (usually two) and important keys (again, usually two) are presented; the *development,* in which the themes are treated in various ways and different keys are explored; the *recapitulation,* a restatement of the exposition with some modifications, mainly in the use of keys. A coda may be added. *See* coda.

style (p. 20) In music, style refers to the unique way in which the elements of melody, rhythm, and harmony are handled to create a special "sound."

syncopation (p. 24) An arrangement of rhythm in which prominent or important tones begin on weak beats or weak parts of beats, giving a catchy, "off-balance" movement to the music.

system (p. 160) A construction of staffs joined at the left by a vertical line and showing all vocal and instrumental parts being performed. Also called a *score.*

tempo (p. 8) The speed of the beat in a piece of music.

tone painting (p. 40) Music that describes its nonmusical subject; for example, as a piece of music about rain attempts to *sound* like rain.

tone row (p. 71) A prearranged order of the twelve tones of an octave. Tone rows serve as the basis for some types of twentieth-century musical compositions.

trio (p. 118) The contrasting section between the first appearance and the repetition of a minuet. *See* minuet.

tutti (p. 40) An Italian word meaning "all"; used in orchestral works to indicate that a part is to be played by the whole orchestra.

underscore (p. 14) Music that accompanies a dramatic scene; background music for a play, motion picture, or television drama.

whole-tone scale (p. 69) A scale of six different tones, built entirely of whole steps. This scale is usually associated with the music of impressionist composers, especially Claude Debussy. *See* scale.

Can You Read This?

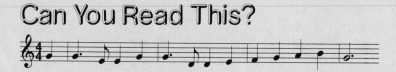

Reading music is a lot like reading words. In words, letters are written down in a way that is meant to represent certain sounds. In the same way, music is a method of writing down sounds. It is a written "musical language."

Sometimes written music looks more complicated to us than written words. When that happens, it is a good idea to look at the written symbols and work out one bit of musical language at a time. In the example of music at the top of this page, we can begin by using what we know about the written *rhythm* of music.

We can begin by clapping or tapping out the rhythm:

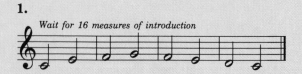

Next we can look for short sections in order to work out the *tonal* language. Does a tonal pattern move up or down? Do any tones repeat? Are the notes close together or do they leap around? Are there patterns that repeat or almost repeat?

Here is a repeated pattern you can sing with the recording of a song in this book. It is short and simple, and because it repeats exactly, it is good practice for beginning music reading. You may remember that these repeated patterns are sometimes called *ostinatos*.

1.

Wait for 16 measures of introduction

Here is a different *ostinato* for the same song. How is it different?

2.

Reference Bank

Here is a melody you can read and then sing with the recording of
the song in this book. It is longer and more complicated than the
ostinatos on the preceeding page. However, you can make it easier
by taking it apart. Clap the rhythm first. Look for tonal patterns.
Then sing the song in short sections before putting it all together.

3.

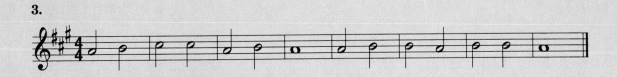

Here is a slightly more complicated melody to read and sing with
the same song. Does it move mostly by step or mostly by leap?   (By step.)

4.

Melodic leaps make this melody challenging to read. If you look for
patterns that repeat, it will be easier.

Even though the pattern of this melody is quite different from the
two others on this page, it will still work with the song we have
been using.

5.

Reference Bank

Here are more melodies for practicing music reading. Each one will harmonize with a song in this book.

In this next melody, look for repeating patterns. Some repeat exactly. Others are similar or repeat only the rhythm and contour of the melody. Notice that it begins with a "pickup" note.

6.

This melody moves mostly by step. However, no section repeats exactly. Read a few measures at a time before putting it all together.

7.

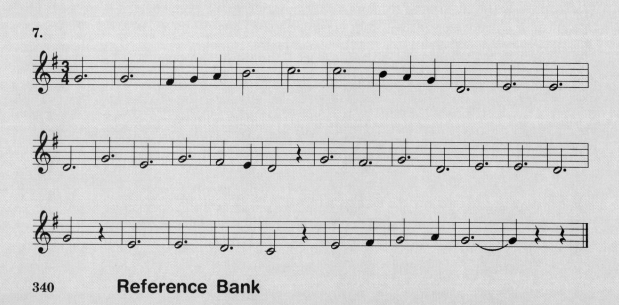

Reference Bank

Melodic leaps make this melody challenging to read. However, if you
look for the patterns that repeat, it will be easier.

8.

This melody has a new element of musical language to read. Be sure
to repeat the section that is marked with :‖ or it won't come out even
when it is sung with the recording. (Watch out for the "pickup" *rest*.)

9.

This melody can be read and sung with a well-known folk song.
(Notice the "pickup" note.)

The third measure from the end may be a little tricky. Why will you
have to be careful when you come to this part?

10.

In the previous song there was a *rest* at the beginning of a measure.
It made that measure more difficult at first. This melody has
several rests in different places and on different beats in the
measure. Remember to take the melody apart, working on small
sections at first. This will make reading it easier.

11.

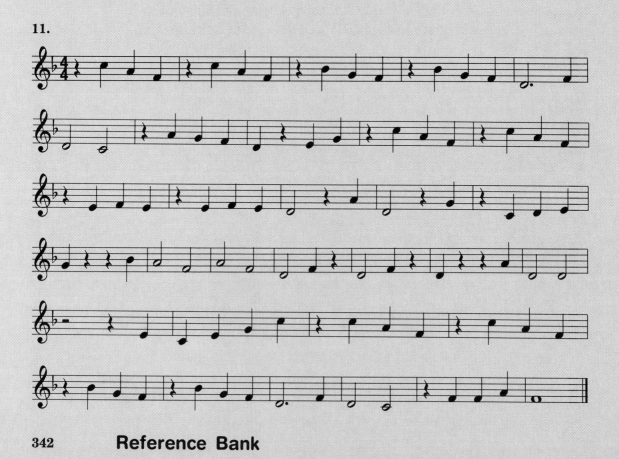

The Sound Bank

Bassoon A large, tube-shaped wooden wind instrument. The player blows into the double reed to make the sound, and presses keys to cover holes in the side of the instrument to change the pitch.
• In the low register the bassoon can sound gruff or comical. The higher notes can be sweet and soft. (p. 107)

Cello A large string instrument made of wood. It is played with a bow, or plucked with the fingers. The cello player sits with the cello between his knees and reaches around the front to play.
• The sound of the cello is rich and warm, but it can sound gruff in the lower register and very intense in the higher register. (p. 52)

Clarinet A cylinder-shaped wind instrument, usually wooden but sometimes metal or plastic, with a single reed in the mouthpiece. The player blows into the mouthpiece to make the sound and changes the pitch by pressing keys to cover holes in the side of the instrument.
• The clarinet has three "voices." The lower register is soft and hollow-sounding. The middle register is clear and bright, and the highest notes are more intense and can be very piercing. (p. 25)

English Horn A wooden instrument shaped like a cylinder with a bulb-shaped bell at the bottom. It has a double reed which the player blows into to make the sound. Keys on the side of the instrument are pressed to change the pitch.
• The sound of the English horn is similar to the exotic "oriental" tone color of the oboe, but its "voice" is lower and the tone is richer and warmer. (p. 107)

Flute A small metal instrument shaped like a round piece of pipe. The player blows across an open mouthpiece in the side of the flute near one end, and presses button-like keys to change pitches. Originally flutes were made of wood, but most are now metal, some even gold or silver.
• The sound of the flute is pure, clear, and sweet. The lower notes are very soft and gentle; the higher register is brighter and louder. (p. 25)

French Horn A medium-sized brass instrument made of coiled tubing, with a large bell at the end. The player sits with the horn held down near his lap, and keeps one hand in the bell to control the pitch and tone. He *buzzes* his lips against the mouthpiece to make the sound. The pitch is changed by pressing valves in the side of the horn.
• The sound of the French horn is mellow and warm, and not as loud or assertive as the other brass instruments. (p. 52)

Harpsichord A small keyboard instrument, shaped something like a piano. When the keys are pressed, the strings inside the instrument are plucked by small points of quill, leather or plastic. The harpsichord was popular from about 1550 until 1750, and they have again become widely heard in our own century, even occasionally in popular music.
• Because the strings are plucked, not "hammered" like piano strings, the sound of the harpsichord is light and percussive, with a tinkling, airy quality. It is never very loud, unless it is amplified electronically. (p. 38)

Oboe A small wooden cylinder-shaped instrument. The player blows into a double reed to make the sound, and changes pitch by pressing keys to cover holes in the side of the instrument.
• The sound of the oboe is thin and sweet, often sounding exotic or melancholy. Unlike many other woodwind instruments, the sound gets sweeter and softer as it goes higher. (p. 38)

Piccolo A very small flute. The word *piccolo* in Italian means "little." Piccolos can be made of wood, but are usually metal.
• The high, often shrill sound of the piccolo can be very bird-like. In its lower, softer voice it can sound very sweet and clear. (p. 55)

Recorder A simple wooden flute dating back to the Middle Ages. It is sounded by blowing into a "whistle" mouthpiece at one end. Holes in the side of the recorder are covered and uncovered to change the pitches.
• The recorder has a delicate, quiet tone, even in its more piercing higher register. The recorder comes in many sizes, the larger ones sounding lower, the smaller ones higher. (p. 25)

String Bass (Bass Viol) A large wooden string instrument which is either bowed or plucked. The string bass is taller than most players, who must stand up or sit on a tall stool to play it.
• The sound of the string bass is very dark and resonant, particularly in the lower notes. The strong plucked notes are very useful for establishing a strong "beat," both in classical music and popular music. (p. 90)

Synthesizer A keyboard instrument with keys like a piano which produces sound by means of electronic oscillators. Synthesizers come in all shapes and sizes. Each kind is capable of making a different combination of sounds, though many of the "standard" sounds are similar on all the synthesizers.
• The synthesizer can sound like an electronic version of almost any of the standard orchestral instruments. It also has a range of unusual tone qualities and sound effects, like whistling wind or the popping of popcorn. (p. 76)

Trombone A fairly large brass instrument with a large bell at the end of the tubing. The sound is made by *buzzing* the lips against the mouthpiece. The pitches are changed by pushing and pulling a metal "slide," lengthening and shortening the tubing.
• The trombone can sound very aggressive and noisy; but in its softer "voice" it can be warm and mellow. (p. 25)

Trumpet A small brass instrument with a bell at one end of its coiled tubing. The player *buzzes* his lips against the mouthpiece to make the sound, and changes pitch by pushing button-shaped valves on the top of the instrument.
• The sound of the trumpet is bold and bright, but it can sound sweet, even melancholy when playing a lyrical melody. (p. 107)

Tuba A very large brass instrument with a wide bell, usually facing upward, at the end. The player *buzzes* his lips against the mouthpiece to make the sound, and changes pitch by pushing valves on the side of the coiled tubing.
• The tuba's sound is low and sturdy. It can keep a rhythm pattern by playing short, regularly-spaced notes. However, it sometimes plays a melody, and is surprisingly rich and mellow-sounding. (p. 55)

Viola A wooden string instrument which looks like a large violin. The viola is either bowed or plucked.
• The sound of the viola is lower and darker than the violin. (p. 52)

Violin A small wooden string instrument. The violin is held under the player's chin. The strings are plucked or bowed with the player's right hand, and the pitches are changed by pressing the strings with the fingers of the left hand.
• The violin has a number of very different "voices." It has a wide range of notes, from medium low to very high, and the tone quality can vary from a liquid "singing" sound to a harsh, angry, raspy sound, and many others in between. (p. 38)

Classified Index

LISTENING LIBRARY

The following selections are heard in their entirety.

LYRICS

THEME MUSICAL

Song Index

Picture Credits

Acknowledgments

The authors and editors acknowledge with gratitude the assistance of Mr. James Kaina, Hawaii Visitors Bureau, New York City, in researching the song "Say Good-by to These Islands" *("Ku'u Ipo Ika He'e Pueone")*

The editors of Silver Burdett & Ginn have made every attempt to verify the source of "Hwi Ne Ya He," but were unable to do so. We believe this chant to be in the public domain.